No Turning Back

A GUIDE TO THE 1864 OVERLAND CAMPAIGN, FROM THE WILDERNESS TO COLD HARBOR, MAY 4 - JUNE 13, 1864

By Robert M. Dunkerly,
Donald C. Pfanz, and David R. Ruth

EMERGING CIVIL WAR SERIES

Chris Mackowski, series editor
Christopher Kolakowski, chief historian

The Emerging Civil War Series

offers compelling, easy-to-read overviews of some of the Civil War's most important battles and stories.

Recipient of the Army Historical Foundation's Lieutenant General Richard G. Trefry Award for contributions to the literature on the history of the U.S. Army

Also part of the Emerging Civil War Series:

Embattled Capital: A Guide to Richmond During the Civil War by Robert M. Dunkerly and Doug Crenshaw

The Last Road North: A Guide to the Gettysburg Campaign, 1863 by Robert Orrison and Dan Welch

To Hazard All: A Guide to the 1862 Maryland Campaign by Robert Orrison and Kevin Pawlak

Hell Itself: The Battle of the Wilderness, May 5-7, 1864 by Chris Mackowski

A Season of Slaughter: The Battle of Spotsylvania Court House, May 8-21, 1864 by Chris Mackowski and Kristopher D. White

Strike Them a Blow: Battle Along the North Anna River, May 21-25, 1864 by Chris Mackowski

Hurricane from the Heavens: The Battle of Cold Harbor, May 26-June 5, 1864 by Daniel T. Davis and Phillip S. Greenwalt

The Aftermath of Battle: The Burial of the Civil War Dead by Meg Groeling

To the Bitter End: Appomattox, Bennett Place, and the Surrenders of the Confederacy by Robert M. Dunkerly

For a complete list of titles in the Emerging Civil War Series,
visit www.emergingcivilwar.com

No Turning Back

A Guide To the 1864 Overland Campaign, From the Wilderness to Cold Harbor, May 4 - June 13, 1864

By Robert M. Dunkerly,
Donald C. Pfanz, and David R. Ruth

SB
Savas Beatie
California

Third edition, first printing

ISBN-13: 978-1-61121-193-1

Library of Congress Cataloging-in-Publication Data

Dunkerly, Robert M.
No turning back : a guide to the 1864 Overland Campaign, from the Wilderness to Cold Harbor, May 4-June 13, 1864 / by Robert M. Dunkerly, Donald C. Pfanz, and David R. Ruth.
pages cm. -- (Emerging Civil War series)
Includes bibliographical references.
ISBN 978-1-61121-193-1
1. Overland Campaign, Va., 1864. 2. United States--History--Civil War, 1861-1865--Campaigns. 3. Virginia--History--Civil War, 1861-1865--Campaigns. 4. Virginia-
-History--Civil War, 1861-1865--Battlefields--Guidebooks. I. Pfanz, Donald. II. Ruth, David R. III. Title.
E476.52.D86 2014
975.5'03--dc23
2014005096

Published by
Savas Beatie LLC
989 Governor Drive, Suite 102
El Dorado Hills, California 95762
Phone: 916-941-6896
Email: sales@savasbeatie.com
Web: www.savasbeatie.com

Savas Beatie titles are available at special discounts for bulk purchases in the United States by corporations, institutions, and other organizations. For more details, please contact Special Sales, P.O. Box 4527, El Dorado Hills, CA 95762, or you may e-mail us as at sales@savasbeatie.com, or visit our website at www.savasbeatie.com for additional information.

For Chris Catalfamo and the others who have inspired us

Table of Contents

The James River—site of the pontoon bridge Federal engineers built on June 14, 1864. (RD)

List of Maps

Maps by Hal Jespersen

Acknowledgments

It takes the talents of many people to produce a book. The authors wish to acknowledge help they received from the folks at Savas Beatie, particularly Dr. Chris Mackowski, who shepherded the manuscript through the publishing process. Cartographer Hal Jespersen produced the fine maps that appear in this volume, many of which appeared in earlier books written by Chris Mackowski, Kris White, Daniel Davis, and Phillip Greenwalt, who kindly allowed us to use them. Finally, we would be remiss if we did not acknowledge too the role played by our friend Don Pierce. A key figure in establishing the Virginia Civil War Trails system, it was Don's idea to produce this companion guide. To him and to all the others mentioned here, we thank you.

Confederate artillery near the visitor contact station at Cold Harbor (CM)

In addition, the authors would like to extend personal thank yous to the following groups and individuals:

ROBERT: The mark of a good historian is not only one who researches thoroughly but who also shares. My understanding of the Cold Harbor campaign has deepened through the generosity of Bob Krick. He patiently tolerated "just one more question" and I value our many hikes through the uncharted woods and fields of the battlefield.

My parents took me on many vacations to the historic sites of Virginia; I thank them for investing the time and effort to satisfy my curiosity to see these places. They were always willing to make "just one more stop."

Chris Catalfamo was an inspiring teacher who led by example. I am grateful to have learned from her.

There are a group of passionate people in the northwest corner of Connecticut who have shared their enthusiasm for the region's Cold Harbor connections with me. They include Ed and Ruth Epstein, Blair and Mary Lou Pavlik, John and Jane Bonville, Pete Vermilyea, the members of Post 27 American Legion of Litchfield, and the various historical societies of Litchfield County.

My co-authors, Dave and Don, kept me on track and made suggestions that produced a better work than I would have otherwise. Their passion for preservation and research is inspiring.

DAVE: Special thanks is due to several individuals who provided both inspiration and immense aid to me in compiling information for this book. Mrs. Dorothy Francis Atkinson graciously invited me into her home, "Wyoming," and shared her family's story from May 1864, as well as her vast knowledge of the historic roads of Hanover and King William County. Historian Bobby Krick's indefatigable assistance with gathering and assessing historical manuscripts is legendary and his help was very much appreciated by this author. Thanks also to Gordon Rhea and photo historian Mike Gorman for their insight and support.

Finally, I am deeply grateful to my wife, Chris, for her companionship, constant stream of encouragement, and tremendous patience in everything that I do.

DON: I wish to thank my friends and former colleagues Courtney Moose, Eric Mink, Jenny Griffith, and Noel Harrison for patiently helping me, giving me access to their offices, and helping me to track down photographs and quotations for this book.

PHOTO CREDITS:
Chris Mackowski (CM);
Donald Pfanz (DP);
Fredericksburg &
Spotsylvania National Military
Park (FSNMP);
Library of Congress (LOC):
Robert Dunkerly (RD)

Looking downriver from Ox Ford at the North Anna River (CM)

For the Emerging Civil War Series

Theodore Savas, publisher
Chris Mackowski, series editor
Christopher Kolakowski, chief historian
Sarah Keeney, editorial consultant

Maps by Hal Jespersen
Design and layout by Chris Mackowski
Kristopher D. White, editor emeritus

Touring the Battlefields

Over the past 20 years, the Commonwealth of Virginia has created a series of driving tours covering major Civil War campaigns fought in the state. Called "Virginia Civil War Trails," the tours include such epic struggles as the 1862 Peninsula campaign, Lee's retreat to Appomattox, various battle sites in Northern Virginia, and both the 1862 and 1864 Shenandoah Valley campaigns. Among the earliest tour routes created was "Lee vs. Grant: The 1864 Campaign," which follows the Union and Confederate armies as they battled one another step by step from the Wilderness to Petersburg. This guide compliments that trail, providing additional information at many of the stops and adding a few stops not found on the state-sponsored trail. Taken together, the Lee vs. Grant trail signs and the information provided by this guide provide a comprehensive view of the campaign and take readers to spots pivotal to the campaign that they might not otherwise visit.

Massaponax Church (CM)

Although this guide generally follows the Lee vs. Grant trail, there are a few side trips to "optional" stops, so please be sure to consult the written directions to each stop in addition to using the Virginia Civil War Trails signs. GPS coordinates are also provided for each stop. Although maps in this guide will help you navigate the tour route, you may also wish to consult the campaign map provided in the Lee vs. Grant tour pamphlet, a free

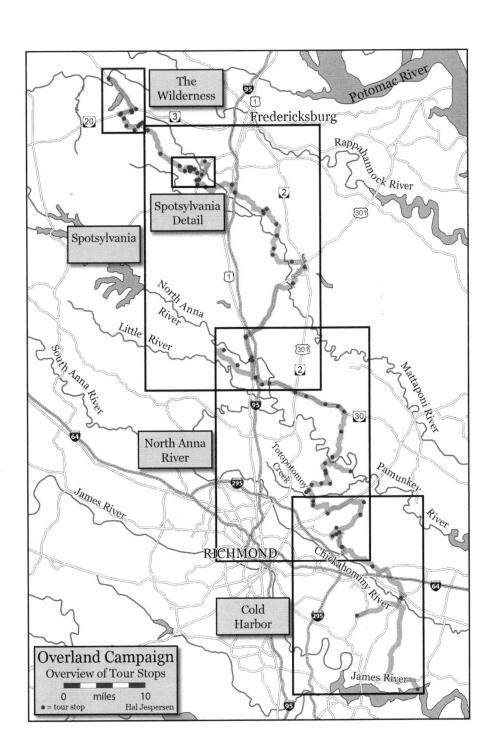

The Wilderness

Fredericksburg

Potomac River

Rappahannock River

Spotsylvania Detail

Spotsylvania

North Anna River

Little River

South Anna River

Mattaponi River

North Anna River

Totopotomoy Creek

Pamunkey River

RICHMOND

Chickahominy River

Cold Harbor

James River

James River

Overland Campaign
Overview of Tour Stops

0   miles   10

● = tour stop   Hal Jespersen

Mount Carmel Church (CM)

copy of which you can get by calling 1-888-CIVILWAR. Be aware that the tour route is approximately 120 miles in length. Allow yourself two days to cover it all, or even three if you plan to read historical signs along the way or hike some of the trails.

Important preservation work by the Central Virginia Battlefields Trust, Civil War Trust, Blue and Gray Education Society, and Richmond Battlefield Association has saved many of these properties and made them available to you. We encourage you to support their work. In some instances, this tour will pass properties that are privately owned. Please do not trespass.

Keep in mind that some roads are one way, and others may have heavy traffic. At times, you will be driving through neighborhoods and towns. Please follow all speed limits and park only in areas that are both safe and legal. Enjoy your tour!

BATTLEFIELD PRESERVATION ORGANIZATIONS

Civil War Trust
156 15th Street NW, Suite 900
Washington, D.C. 20005
202-367-1861
www.civilwar.org

Central Virginia Battlefields Trust
2217 Princess Anne Street
Fredericksburg, Virginia 22401
540-374-9000
www.cvbt.org

Richmond Battlefields Association
P.O. Box 13945
Richmond, Virginia 23225
804-496-1862
www.saverichmondbattlefields.org

Blue & Gray Education Society
P.O. Box 1176
Chatham, Virginia 24531-1176
434-250-9921
www.blueandgrayeducation.org

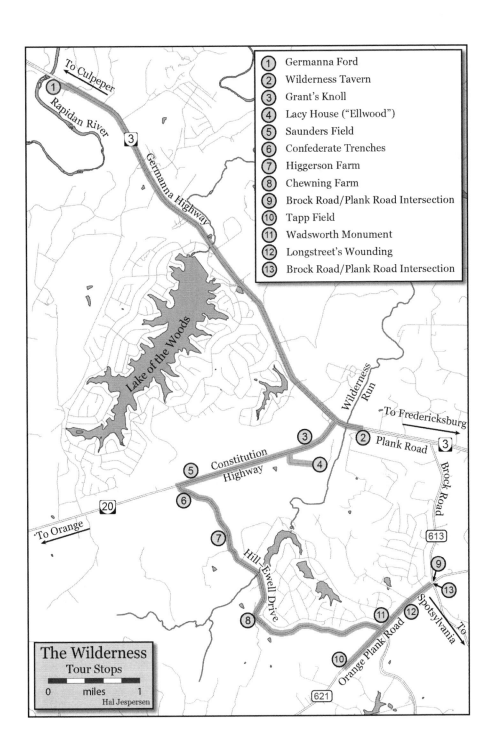

The Wilderness
Tour Stops

1. Germanna Ford
2. Wilderness Tavern
3. Grant's Knoll
4. Lacy House ("Ellwood")
5. Saunders Field
6. Confederate Trenches
7. Higgerson Farm
8. Chewning Farm
9. Brock Road/Plank Road Intersection
10. Tapp Field
11. Wadsworth Monument
12. Longstreet's Wounding
13. Brock Road/Plank Road Intersection

Hal Jespersen

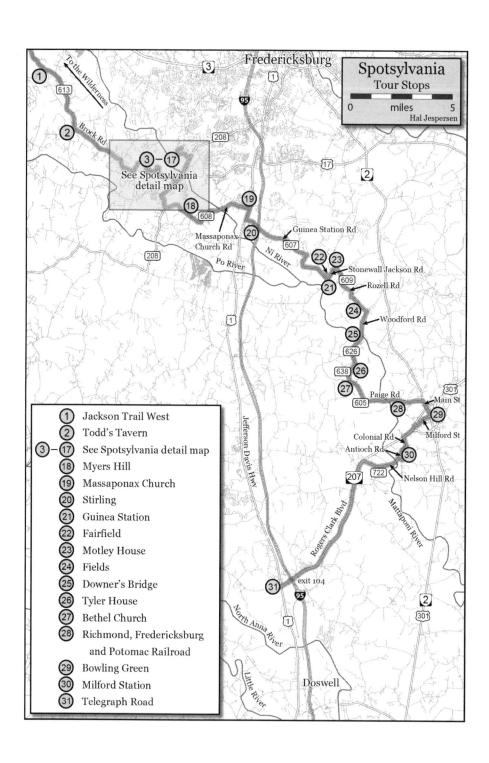

Spotsylvania
Tour Stops

0   miles   5
Hal Jespersen

① Jackson Trail West
② Todd's Tavern
③–⑰ See Spotsylvania detail map
⑱ Myers Hill
⑲ Massaponax Church
⑳ Stirling
㉑ Guinea Station
㉒ Fairfield
㉓ Motley House
㉔ Fields
㉕ Downer's Bridge
㉖ Tyler House
㉗ Bethel Church
㉘ Richmond, Fredericksburg
    and Potomac Railroad
㉙ Bowling Green
㉚ Milford Station
㉛ Telegraph Road

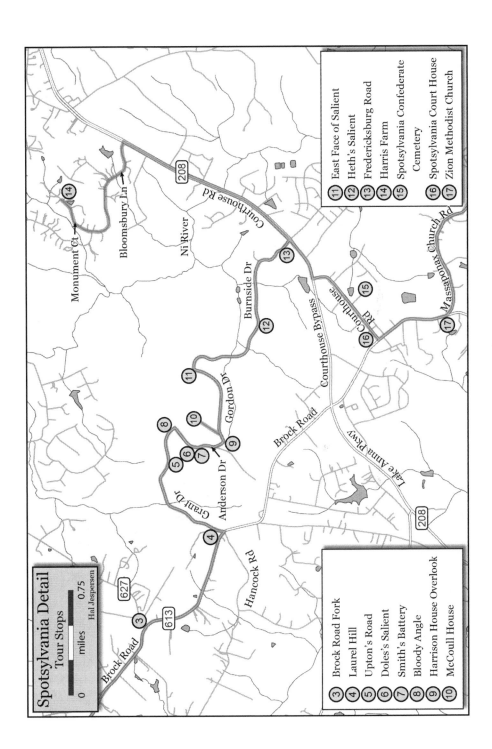

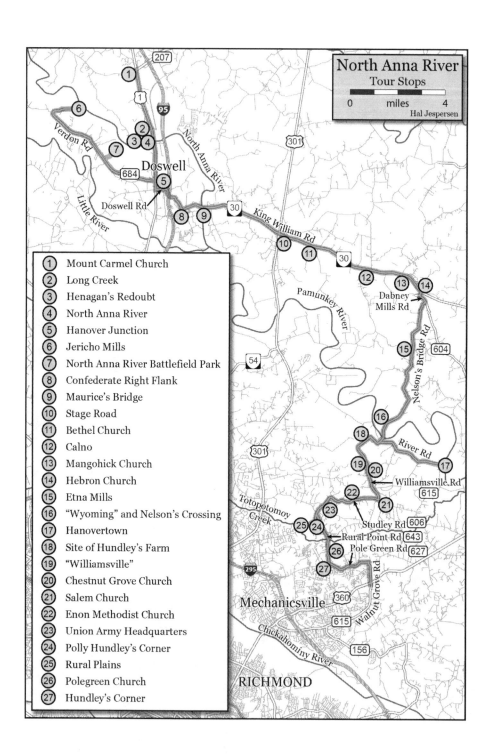

North Anna River
Tour Stops

0   miles   4
Hal Jespersen

1. Mount Carmel Church
2. Long Creek
3. Henagan's Redoubt
4. North Anna River
5. Hanover Junction
6. Jericho Mills
7. North Anna River Battlefield Park
8. Confederate Right Flank
9. Maurice's Bridge
10. Stage Road
11. Bethel Church
12. Calno
13. Mangohick Church
14. Hebron Church
15. Etna Mills
16. "Wyoming" and Nelson's Crossing
17. Hanovertown
18. Site of Hundley's Farm
19. "Williamsville"
20. Chestnut Grove Church
21. Salem Church
22. Enon Methodist Church
23. Union Army Headquarters
24. Polly Hundley's Corner
25. Rural Plains
26. Polegreen Church
27. Hundley's Corner

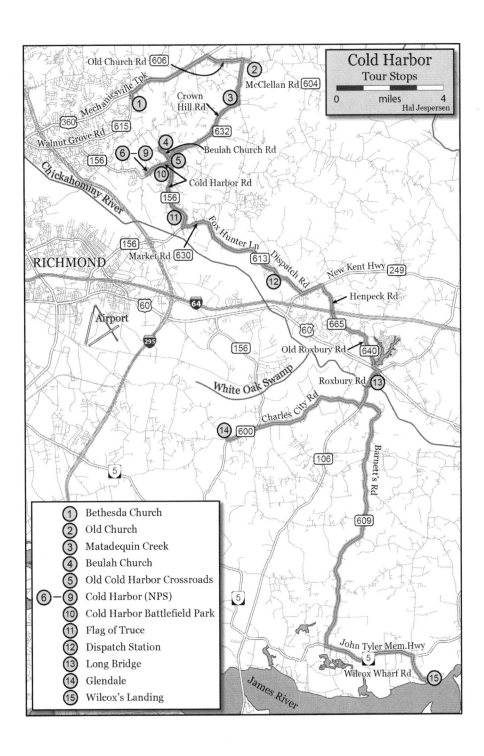

"Well, if you see the President, tell him from me that, whatever happens, there will be no turning back."

— *Lt. Gen. Ulysses S. Grant*
May 5, 1864

Prelude to the Campaign

April 1864 ushered in the fourth year of the American Civil War. Gone were the hopeful days of 1861, when citizens of both the North and South predicted a quick and decisive end to the conflict. Gone too were the days when news of defeat cast a nation into gloom or news of victory lifted it to giddy heights of optimism. The people in both sections of the country had matured, just as the armies that defended them had matured. Victory, they realized, would not be won in a single day, nor on a single battlefield, but instead would be the culmination of dozens of bloody fights, large and small, across the continent.

Both sides sensed that the 1864 campaign would be decisive. In the North it was an election year. In November, the citizens would cast their ballots, voting either to sustain President Abraham Lincoln in his efforts to restore the Union or to elect a candidate who would try to negotiate a peace predicated on Southern independence. Which way the people voted would depend in large measure on whether Lincoln and his generals could show solid progress toward ending the rebellion before Northern voters headed to the polls.

Lincoln fully understood the importance of the upcoming campaign. To increase the chances for victory, in March he appointed Lt. Gen. Ulysses S. Grant to head the Union war effort. Up to that time, Grant had been a successful commander in the west; now Lincoln placed him in command of

The Bloody Angle at Spotsylvania is one of many landscapes indelibly written into American history because of Grant's Overland Campaign.
(Opposite page: DP; previous spread CM)

"I can't spare Grant. He fights," President Abraham Lincoln (left) once said of Ulysses S. Grant (right). In the spring of 1864, Lincoln counted on Grant's fighting spirit when he promoted Grant to the rank of lieutenant general and appointed him to command all Federal armies. (LOC)

Union armies throughout the country. Grant chose to make his headquarters with his largest force, Maj. Gen. George G. Meade's Army of the Potomac. For three years, the Army of the Potomac had battled Gen. Robert E. Lee in Virginia, Maryland, and Pennsylvania; except at Gettysburg, it had seldom achieved victory. By making his headquarters with Meade, Grant hoped to infuse the army with his own relentless drive and determination, and forge victories with an army that had hitherto known little but defeat.

The soldiers in the Army of the Potomac received the news of Grant's arrival coolly. Although they were aware of Grant's success in the West, fighting Lee was another matter. Thomas Walter of the 91st Pennsylvania confessed: "General Meade we knew pretty well, and had a good deal of confidence in, but the matter of General Grant assuming the chief directorship of the Army of the Potomac did not strike us very favorably." Colonel Seldon Conner of the 7th Maine reflected the army's wait-and-see attitude. "There is no enthusiasm for Gen. Grant," he wrote, "and on the other hand, there is no prejudice against him. We are prepared to throw up our hats when he shows himself the great soldier in Virginia against Lee and the best troops of the rebels."

The Army of the Potomac left its winter camps in Culpeper County, Virginia, on May 4 and crossed the Rapidan River, embarking on a six-week campaign that would not end until it stood at the gates of Petersburg. This booklet will take you on a detailed driving tour of that campaign. As you take this tour, you will drive the same roads once trodden by the men of Grant's and Lee's armies. You will pass quiet intersections that once echoed the roar of battle. You will see buildings that generals used as headquarters and stand on ground hallowed by more than a dozen bloody battles and skirmishes. Most important, you will gain a greater appreciation of the Overland campaign—a campaign that helped secure the reelection of Abraham Lincoln and, in doing so, sealed the doom of the Confederacy.

Grant made his headquarters in the field with Maj. Gen. George Gordon Meade's Army of the Potomac. Since his victory at Gettysburg in July of 1863, Meade (left) had grappled with Gen. Robert E. Lee (right) and the Army of Northern Virginia in a back-and-forth struggle that left Meade unable to deliver a knockout. (LOC)

The Wilderness

CHAPTER ONE

MAY 3-7, 1864

"It was like . . . the wildest regions of 'Dante's Inferno.' The forest which once covered the entire section with a magnificent growth had been cut over repeatedly to furnish fuel for the mines which had been worked in the vicinity since the first habitation of the region, and instead of the natural growth there had sprung up everywhere a dense thicket of scrub pine, oak and walnut saplings, hazel and other bushes and briars, so dense that it was next to impossible to force one's way through them without the loss of cap and the tearing of clothing. Interspersed with rocky tracts on which only a gymnast could maintain his footing were marshes even more impassable." Thus Priv. James L. Bowen of the 37th Massachusetts described the Wilderness, a tract of tangled, second growth forest 70 square miles in extent that stretched south of the Rapidan River toward Spotsylvania Court House. In this forbidding setting would be fought one of the great battles of the Civil War—the first test of strength between the war's two foremost military leaders, Gens. Ulysses S. Grant and Robert E. Lee.

Just 42 years old at the time the campaign began, Grant in just two years' time had won victories at Fort Henry, Fort Donelson, Shiloh, Chattanooga, and Vicksburg. Now general in chief of Union armies throughout the nation, he planned to use the North's superior numbers to crush the rebellion. While Maj. Gen. William Tecumseh Sherman struck toward Atlanta and the Confederate heartland and Gen. Nathaniel

Banks operated against Confederate forces along the Gulf Coast, Union armies in Virginia would strangle Richmond into submission. The largest of these, Meade's Army of the Potomac, would drive south from Culpeper, engaging Lee in or near the Wilderness. With Lee pinned down in north-central Virginia, Maj. Gen. Benjamin F. Butler's Army of the James would be free to sweep up the James River and capture Richmond from the rear. At the same time, Maj. Gen. Franz Sigel would work his way up the Shenandoah Valley, farther to the west, cutting railroads and destroying crops, denying Lee's army the sustenance it needed to survive. It was an excellent plan but failed when both Butler and Sigel suffered defeat at the hands of smaller Confederate forces. With their defeats, responsibility for capturing Richmond fell to Meade and the Army of the Potomac. The campaign would begin at Germanna Ford.

To reach Germanna Ford, the first stop on the Lee vs. Grant Trail, take I-95 to Exit 130B. That will put you on State Route 3 heading west. Follow Route 3 for 17.4 miles. Turn left onto the Locust Grove campus of Germanna Community College. Then take your first right and park at the Germanna Visitor Center. Signs for the Lee vs. Grant Trail are adjacent to the parking lot.

GPS N 38°.224092 W 77°.470104

STOP 1: GERMANNA FORD

The Union army crossed the Rapidan River at Germanna Ford. (LOC)

Grant's instructions to Meade at the outset of the Overland Campaign were short and to the point: "Lee's army will be your objective point. Wherever Lee goes, there you will go also." The Confederate army had spent the winter camped here, in Orange County. To get at it, Meade would have to cross the Rapidan River, which for five months had formed a watery boundary between the two armies. Rather than make a frontal assault against Lee defenses, Meade chose to cross here at Germanna Ford and turn the Confederate leader's right flank.

At dawn, May 4, Brig. Gen. James H. Wilson's Union cavalry division splashed across the ford, scattering the small number of Confederate pickets standing guard here. Union engineers quickly threw two pontoon bridges across the river, and Maj. Gen. Gouverneur K. Warren's V Corps began to cross. Grant and Meade watched the crossing from a bluff overlooking the ford. With them stood Lt. Col. Theodore Lyman, Meade's aide-de-camp. The thought of the carnage that would soon ensue weighed heavily on Lyman's mind. As he gazed upon the unending procession crossing the river, a morbid thought entered his head. "How strange it would be," he mused, "if each man who was destined to fall in the campaign had some large badge on!"

Death of a different sort preyed on the mind of Lt. Col. Edwin C. Mason of the 5th Maine. With Grant at Germanna Ford was Elihu B. Washburne, a Congressman from Grant's own district in Illinois. Dressed in a black suit and a stovepipe hat, Washburne attracted the notice of troops marching past. Some joked that Grant had brought his own private undertaker with him, while others jested that "it was a parson who had joined headquarters so as to be on hand to read the funeral service over the Southern Confederacy . . . ."

May 4 ended with the Army of the Potomac safely across the Rapidan River. For Grant, successful passage of the river was reason to celebrate. He had feared that Lee would contest the crossing, and when the Confederate leader did not, it put Grant in a good humor. When a reporter ventured to ask him how long it would take him to reach Richmond, the Union commander replied: "I will agree to be there in about four days." The reporter's jaw dropped in disbelief, whereat the general added, with a twinkle in his eye, "That is, if General Lee becomes a party to the agreement, but if he objects, the trip will undoubtedly be prolonged."

Information about the history of this site is available at the Germanna Visitor Center. At the far end of the parking lot is a circular drive for turning around. Branching off the drive is a gravel road that leads down to the river, to a point just a few hundred yards upstream from Germanna Ford. From the parking lot, it is approximately a 500-yard walk to the river. Once you have finished exploring this site, return to Route 3.

Lt. Col. Theodore Lyman served on Meade's staff. (LOC)

Most of the fighting in the Wiilderness took place in dense thickets. (FSNMP)

Turn right and drive 4.6 miles to the stoplight at Constitution Highway (Route 20), formerly the Orange Turnpike. If you wish to visit the ruins of Wilderness Tavern, pass through the light and proceed one-quarter mile farther to Lyons Lane, on the right near the crest of the hill. Be alert, as the road is hidden from view. Halt in front of the chimney ruins you find there. That will be stop 2.

GPS N 38°.192874 W 77°.432184.

STOP 2: WILDERNESS TAVERN

Wilderness Tavern (FSNMP)

You are now at the site of Wilderness Tavern, which stood at the junction of the Orange Turnpike (modern Route 20) and the Germanna Plank Road (modern Route 3). Wilson's cavalry reached this point on the morning of May 4. Turning west, it headed along the Orange Turnpike to screen the Army of the Potomac's advance. A few hours later, Warren's V Corps arrived. Although several hours of daylight remained, Warren halted his corps here so as not to outmarch the army's cumbersome wagon train.

The dirt road that you see here is the original Orange Turnpike. Walk down the road to the bottom of the hill. Grant's and Meade's headquarters wagons parked here, in the low ground adjoining Wilderness Run. Just around the road bend is a narrow drive bordered by cedars. This is the historic trace of the Germanna Plank Road. As you can see, it has changed little in 150 years.

Gouverneur Warren reached this intersection around midday, May 4. The swarthy New Yorker commanded one of four corps in Meade's army. Just 34 years of age, Warren was six years younger than Winfield S. Hancock, commander of the army's II Corps and a full 17 years younger than John Sedgwick, the affable leader of Meade's VI Corps. Short, barrel-chested Phil Sheridan commanded the army's cavalry. Brought east by Grant, the pugnacious Sheridan mirrored his chief's aggressive combat style.

Independent of the Army of the Potomac but working in tandem with it was Maj. Gen. Ambrose E. Burnside's IX Corps, which reached Virginia just as the campaign was about to get underway. The likeable but hapless Burnside had been the army's commander back in 1862 but had been replaced by Lincoln following the disastrous battle at Fredericksburg. Following a stint in the Midwest, he returned to Virginia in command of the IX Corps, the same unit he had led prior to his promotion to army command. Although the same rank as Meade, Burnside's had received his commission as major general prior to Meade, technically making him Meade's superior, even though Burnside commanded a smaller force. To prevent friction between the two men, Grant allowed Burnside to remain independent of Meade. For the first few weeks of the campaign, until he voluntarily subordinated himself to Meade's authority, Burnside received orders directly from Grant himself.

Looking west down the Orange Turnpike from Wilderness Tavern. The view is virtually the same today. (FSNMP)

Altogether the Army of the Potomac, including Burnside's independent IX Corps, entered the campaign with 120,000 men, giving it nearly a two-to-one advantage in numbers over Gen. Robert E. Lee and his Army of Northern Virginia. Like Meade, the Southern commander had divided his army into four corps, three infantry and one cavalry. Dependable James Longstreet, Lee's warhorse, had returned from duty in Eastern Tennessee and would lead his old First Corps in action. One-legged Dick Ewell retained the mantle of command he had inherited from "Stonewall" Jackson a year earlier and would be marching at the head of the army's Second Corps, while feisty but temperamental A. P. Hill had charge of Lee's Third Corps. Thirty-three-year-old J. E. B. Stuart, Lee's playful but competent cavalier, commanded the South's cavalry. Lee's command structure was short lived. By the time the campaign ended, Stuart would be dead, Longstreet seriously wounded, and Ewell transferred because of debility. Of the four corps commanders, only A. P. Hill—himself suffering from chronic disease—

Thousands of soldiers marched down this remnant of the Germanna Plank Road—now a private driveway. (DP)

would still be with the army when it crossed the James River six weeks later.

Return to your vehicle and continue east (right) on Route 3. Get in the left lane and make a U-turn at your first opportunity. Return to the stoplight at Constitution Highway (Route 20) and turn left. Drive less than one-half of a mile to a pull-off on the right.

GPS N 38°.191991 W 77°.440239

STOP 3: GRANT'S KNOLL

For three days, General Grant and General Meade made their headquarters here on a small rise beside the Orange Turnpike. A soldier observed the two generals in consultation on the bare hill. "The small form with the slight stoop in the shoulders, sunken gray eyes; still, reserved demeanor, impassive face, and chin as of a bull-dog or a close-set steel-trap—that is Grant," he wrote; "the tall figure, with the nervous emphatic articulation and action, the face as of antique parchment—that is Meade—and the antipodes could not bring together a greater contrast."

Grant intended to accompany the Army of the Potomac merely as an observer but that changed as soon as the fighting started. From that point on, Grant and Meade commanded the army in tandem,

General Grant at his Wilderness headquarters. On May 6, he reportedly smoked twenty cigars as he followed the action of the battle. (FSNMP)

in what at first was an awkward and uncomfortable arrangement. One newspaper described the Army of the Potomac as being "directed by Grant, commanded by Meade, and led by Hancock, Sedgwick and Warren," a distinction, thought Meade, which "about hits the nail on the head."

Working in such close proximity gave Meade a good opportunity to size up his new boss. "Grant is not a mighty genius," he wrote his wife, "but he is a good soldier, of great force of character, honest and upright, of pure purposes, I think, without political aspirations, certainly not influenced by them." Meade praised Grant's "tenacity of purpose," which blinded him to obstacles that would have daunted other men. "Take him all in all, he is, in my judgment, the best man the war has yet produced."

Continue west on Constitution Highway (Route 20) for 0.2 mile and turn left into the gravel driveway marked "Ellwood." If the gate is open, drive back to the house. Otherwise, park your car at the gate, being careful not to block the access, and walk the one-third-mile distance to the house.

GPS N 38°.190986 W 77°.435373

STOP 4: THE LACY HOUSE ("ELLWOOD")

This house, which belonged to Confederate Maj. James Horace Lacy, witnessed a great deal of Civil War activity. For several months in 1863, it became a hospital for Confederate soldiers wounded at the battle of Chancellorsville and its cemetery the burial spot for Lt. Gen. Thomas J. "Stonewall" Jackson's amputated arm. General Robert E. Lee pitched his tent at Ellwood in June 1863, on his way to Gettysburg, and six months later Union troops looted the building in their retreat from Mine Run. The house played its greatest role during the battle of the Wilderness, when it served as the headquarters for three different Union generals: Gouverneur Warren, Ambrose Burnside, and Samuel Crawford.

The land around the house was then open,

Three Union generals occupied Ellwood as a headquarters during the battle of the Wilderness, but today it is better remembered as the burial location for "Stonewall" Jackson's amputated arm. (FSNMP)

Ellwood's owner, Maj. James Horace Lacy (FSNMP)

providing an unobstructed view of the Wilderness Run valley. Imagine standing here during the battle and seeing hundreds of supply wagons and ambulances stretched out before you; horses and mules by the thousands; more than a dozen cannon posted in a line along the current driveway. It is no wonder that a Connecticut soldier who had witnessed such great strength felt that such an army "could overcome the world."

Ellwood is open at different times during the year. Paths lead from the yard south to the cemetery, now surrounded by a short post-and-rail fence, and northeast to the site of Wilderness Tavern. Once you have finished touring the site, return to Route 20, turn left, and drive one mile to the Wilderness Exhibit Shelter, on your right. Park in the lot and stand facing west, so that the highway is on your left.

GPS N 38° .190262 W 77° .452388

STOP 5: SAUNDERS FIELD

The first combat in the Wilderness took place here at Saunders field, a small clearing astride the Orange Turnpike. The V Corps was preparing to resume its march through the Wilderness on May 5, when Confederates led by Lt. Gen. Richard S. Ewell appeared at Saunders field. Grant and Meade ordered Warren to attack. The V Corps commander went forward at 1 p.m. His corps swept across this field, striking the Confederate line just inside the edge of the woods, ahead of you. Although

The first fighting of the campaign occurred in Saunders Field. (FSNMP)

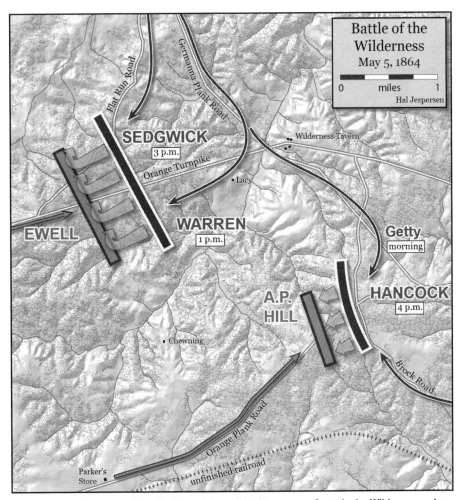

BATTLE OF THE WILDERNESS, MAY 5—General Lee wished to engage Grant in the Wilderness, where the dense woodlands would help negate the Union army's superiority in artillery, cavalry, and infantry. On May 5, the Confederates thundered out of the west, Ewell engaging Warren and Sedgwick along the Orange Turnpike and Hill combating Hancock and Getty on the Plank Road. Ewell turned back the Union assaults in his front with relative ease, while Hill, on the other hand, barely hung on.

Warren broke Ewell's line south of the Turnpike (to your left), a counterattack by Brig. Gen. John Gordon quickly restored the line. Repulsed at all points, Warren spent the rest of the afternoon rallying his shattered command. Meanwhile, Maj. Gen. John Sedgwick appeared with the VI Corps and extended Warren's line into the woods north of Saunders field, to your right. Late that afternoon, Sedgwick too attacked and was beaten back.

Because most of the fighting in the Wilderness took place amid deep woods, soldiers gauged the

Gouverneur Warren's attack at Saunders Field initiated the battle. (LOC)

battle's progress as much by sound as by sight. "The rattle of musketry would swell into a continuous roar as the simultaneous discharge of 10,000 guns mingled in one grand concert, and then after a few minutes, became more interrupted, resembling the crash of some huge king of the forest when felled by the stroke of the woodman's ax," wrote Surgeon George T. Stevens of the 77th New York. "Then would be heard the wild yells which always told of a rebel charge, and again the volleys would swell into one continuous roll of sound, which would presently be interrupted by the vigorous manly cheers of the northern soldiers, so different from the shrill yell of the rebels, and which indicated a repulse of their enemies."

During the night both sides entrenched. Late on May 6, Ewell attacked Sedgwick's right flank in the woods north of the Turnpike. Although the attack created panic in the Union ranks, Sedgwick was able to steady his line and prevent a rout.

Exhibits in this open-air structure provide an overview of the Wilderness fighting. Take a moment and read the exhibits before continuing your tour. A 1.5-mile-long walking trail covering the combat north of the Turnpike begins at the parking lot. When you are ready to move on, turn right out of the parking lot, proceed to the top of the hill, and turn left onto the park tour road, Hill-Ewell Drive. Proceed 200 yards to the tour-stop pull-off, on the right. Walk across the road and follow the short path that leads to the Confederate earthworks.

GPS N 38° .185532 W 77° .452920

STOP 6: CONFEDERATE TRENCHES

The Overland Campaign consisted of as much digging as fighting. In front of you are the remains of once formidable earthworks constructed by Ewell's soldiers. Assistant Surgeon Thomas F. Wood wrote that Southern soldiers, "knowing their weakness, did what they had never done before, built breastworks in front of their lines. It was surprising to see what tools were used. There were not more than two picks to a regiment, and not more than a spade or so, but they improvised tools by bursting a canteen with powder, taking each half for a shovel, either with or without an improvised handle. A bayonet served to loosen the dirt, and the shovels followed after. Our men were good woodcutters and were not slow to fell trees as

Eccentric but capable, Dick Ewell commanded the Confederate Second Corps in the Wilderness. (LOC)

the basis for the works. The practice they were now getting was to serve them for many weary weeks to come, and it was surprising to see how hastily they threw up trenches in a night and even in a few hours."

In the Wilderness, the dry brush combined with the discharge of rifles and the explosion of shells to produce a number of small fires, at least one of which occurred here at Saunders field. A soldier in the Corn Exchange Regiment remembered with horror that as the fires "drew nearer and nearer to the poor unfortunates who lay between the lines, their shrieks, cries and groans, loud, piercing, penetrating, rent the air, until death relieved the sufferer, or the rattle of musketry, that followed the advent of the breaking morn, drowned all the other sounds in its dominating roar. There was no hope of rescue—war's hard rules would not permit it; and there, between the lines, the men of both sides perished in the flames, because there was no helping hand to succor, no yielding to the stern necessities of war."

Confederate earthworks (FSNMP)

Major Wesley Brainerd, a Union engineer engaged in building earthworks near Saunders field, remembered that the dry woods "were fired in a thousand places. The smoke from the clouds of powder and the denser clouds caused by the burning woods became stifling, suffocating, blinding. Two hundred thousand men, inspired with the desperation of demons, were fighting in a wilderness of fire.

"Every moment some souls were leaving that atmosphere of hell, their bodies to be consumed by the devouring elements. Hundreds of wounded on

Fires sparked by muzzle flashes consumed dozens, perhaps hundreds, of wounded soldiers. (FSNMP)

both sides, unable to crawl away from the swiftly approaching flames, could only lay and moan and roast and die."

Continue south along Hill-Ewell Drive two-thirds of a mile to the pull-off for the Higgerson farm, on your right.

GPS N 38° .183083 W 77° .445917

STOP 7: THE HIGGERSON FARM

The Higgerson house (FSNMP)

Although the Wilderness was largely uninhabited, a few hard-working families managed to eke out a living from its thin and unproductive soil. One of these was the Higgersons. Benjamin and Permelia Higgerson raised four children on a small farm located in the fields to your right.

Disaster struck the family on Christmas Day 1862, when Benjamin died of a disease that he had contracted after taking a sick soldier into his house. For Permelia, things only got worse. On May 5, 1864, Union soldiers of Col. Roy Stone's brigade advanced across the Higgerson fields, trampling Permelia's garden and the budding crops in her fields. Undoubtedly, many of her livestock disappeared as well.

Stone's men swept past the Higgerson house only to get bogged down in a waist-deep swamp located in the woods beyond. There they were easy targets for Brig. Gen. Junius Daniel's North Carolinians, who picked them off as they struggled through the mud. In the confusion, some of Stone's men fired into the backs of their comrades who were ahead of them, creating a panic. The entire brigade broke ranks and fled to the rear. Stone, who was drunk that day, rode among his demoralized men, cursing and demanding that they hold their ground. None did. The frightened mob continued its flight until it reached the safety of the Lacy clearing, more than a mile to your left.

From this point a quarter-mile-long trail leads to the site of the Higgerson house, now marked only by the ruins of its chimney. To reach the next stop, the Chewning farm, continue one mile to the pull-off on your right.

GPS N 38° .174525 W 77° .443921

STOP 8: CHEWNING FARM

On the ridge to your right stood the "Mount View," a farm owned by William and Permelia Chewning, an elderly couple who raised wheat, rye, corn, oats, and even tobacco with the help of two grown children and 13 slaves. Situated on high, open ground between the Orange Turnpike and the Orange Plank Road, the 150-acre farm became a point of great tactical importance. If Union troops could occupy the plateau, they would be in position to turn the flanks of both Ewell's Confederates on the Orange Turnpike and Lt. Gen. A. P. Hill's Confederates on the Orange Plank Road. Brigadier General Samuel W. Crawford's Union division occupied the ground early on May 5, but Warren ordered it off the ridge to join the rest of the V Corps in attacking Ewell on the Orange Turnpike. A few hours after Crawford departed, Maj. Gen. Cadmus M. Wilcox's Confederate division occupied the ridge, but it too was called away to support troops in another area.

Union Brig. Gen. Samuel Crawford (above) was the first to occupy the Chewning farm, which was later occupied by Confederate Maj. Gen. Cadmus Wilcox (below). Lt. Gen. A. P. Hill (bottom) came close to being shot there when a line of Federal infantry stumbled upon him and his staff. (LOC)

Recognizing the importance of the ground, Grant ordered Burnside's IX Corps to seize the ridge at dawn on May 6, but Burnside was turned back by a much smaller Confederate force at Jones's field, less than half a mile behind you.

Around midmorning, Hill's corps filed into position here, securing the Chewning farm plateau for the Confederacy. Hill rode ahead of his troops to examine the ground. With him rode his chief of staff, Col. William H. Palmer. "Before the troops came up," remembered Palmer, "we rode to a house and outbuildings in the lower end of the field and dismounted. We had been there only a short while when we were startled by the breaking down of a fence just below, and in plain view was a long line of Federal infantry clearing the fence to move forward. General Hill commanded, 'Mount, walk your horses, and don't look back.'" The party escaped without harm. A few hours later, Hill and his staff rode past a group of Union prisoners, one of whom asked, "Were you not at the house a short time ago?" When Palmer admitted that he was, the man said that he had been there too. "I wanted to fire on you, but my colonel said you were farmers riding from the house."

Hill made the Chewning house his headquarters. On May 7, with the armies at a stalemate, Lee rode to the Chewning farm to confer with him. Again, William Palmer was present. "From the roof some shingles had been broken out, and we had a fine marine glass, and could see clearly the open ground around Wilderness tavern over the tops of the trees. From the constant stream of couriers and officers we felt assured that it was General Grant's headquarters in our view." As Palmer looked on, a large number of batteries left the field and filed into a road heading south. "I went down and reported the movement and direction taken by these heavy guns," wrote Palmer. "It was no doubt simply confirmatory of numerous other reports from the cavalry and other points of the line, that General Grant was moving to Spottsylvania C. H. Orders were at once given for the all-night march . . . ."

The Chewning house no longer stands, but the farm road to your right leads to the site of the building, 360 yards away. To reach the next stop on the driving tour, continue 1.5 miles to the Orange Plank Road, modern Route 621. Turn left and drive three-quarters of a mile to the intersection of the Brock Road (Route 613). Before reaching the intersection, pull into the parking area on the right. Stand facing the intersection with the Plank Road on your left.

GPS N 38° .180289 W 77° .423438

STOP 9: BROCK ROAD/PLANK ROAD INTERSECTION

While Ewell engaged Warren's and Sedgwick's corps in combat along the Orange Turnpike approximately three miles to your left, A. P. Hill's Confederates engaged the rest of the Union army here on the Orange Plank Road. Hill approached the intersection ahead of you around noon on May 5. Had he reached the Brock Road, his corps would have split the Union army in two. But as the Confederates neared the crossroads, Union Brig. Gen. George W. Getty appeared. Getty had orders to seize the intersection and hold it until Maj. Gen. Winfield S. Hancock's corps arrived later in the day. Getty rode to the intersection ahead of his division to survey the situation, arriving just moments ahead of Hill's Confederates. Captain Hazard Stevens,

By his bold actions, General George Getty saved the crossroads for the Union. (LOC)

who was with Getty that day, described the race for the crossroads:

> *Getty instantly hurried back an aide to bring his troops up at the double-quick. Surrounded by his staff and orderlies, with his headquarters flag flying overhead, he took position directly at the intersection of the two roads. Soon a few gray forms were discerned far up the narrow Plank Road moving cautiously forward, then a bullet went whistling overhead, and another and another . . . . Getty would not budge. "We must hold this point at any risk," he exclaimed . . . . In a few minutes, which seemed like an age to the little squad, the leading regiments of Wheaton's brigade . . . came running . . . along the Brock . . . and then at the commands "Halt!" "Front!" "Fire!" poured a volley into the woods and threw out skirmishers in almost less time than it takes to tell it.*

Getty immediately set his troops to work digging entrenchments. For three hours he held the crossroads against Hill's superior force until reinforced by Hancock's II Corps.

Once Hancock arrived, the Union army took the offensive. In some of the most desperate fighting of the war, Hancock and Getty repeatedly assailed Hill's line, hoping to crush the Confederates before night set in. Lieutenant Robert Robertson described the combat: "Now we were in the midst of the din and storm of lead and fire. Only by the flash of the volleys of forming lines could we know where was posted the enemy with which we were engaged. The woods would light up with the flashes of musketry, as if with lightning, while the incessant roar of the volleys sounded like the crashing of thunder-bolts.

The 6th Vermont took heavy casualties in the Wilderness.
(FSNMP)

Brave men were falling like autumn leaves, and death was holding high carnival in our ranks."

In the thickest of the fight was Col. Lewis A. Grant's Vermont Brigade. "We had a terrible battle," wrote the regimental surgeon. "The soldiers were cut down by hundreds. Our Brigade numbering 4000 men when it left camp, now numbers about 700! Our Reg't alone numbered nearly 1000 when it went into the fight and now it numbers 140!"

The Vermont Brigade's casualties might have been even worse, but many of the Confederates fired high. "We were close on to them," remembered Sgt. Wilbur Fisk, "and their fire was terribly effective. Our regiment lost 264 men in killed and wounded. Just a little to the rear of where our line was formed, where the bullets swept close to the ground, every bush and twig was cut and splintered by the leaden balls . . . . I doubt if a single tree could have been found that had not been pierced several times with bullets, and all were hit about breast high. Had the rebels fired a little lower, they would have annihilated the whole line; they nearly did it as it was."

Despite being heavily outnumbered, Hill held his ground until dark. The next morning, however, when Hancock renewed his assault, Hill's line crumbled. As the sun rose over the battlefield, the Army of the Potomac stood on the brink of a brilliant victory.

Turn left out of the parking area and retrace your steps down the Plank Road. After 1.3 miles turn right into a small parking area to the right of the road. Park your vehicle and walk out into the field. Stand next to the cannon and face east, so that the Plank Road is on your right.

The Tapp house (FSNMP)

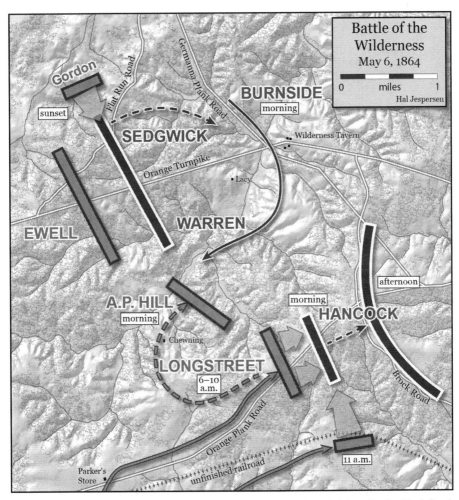

BATTLE OF THE WILDERNESS, MAY 6—May 6 was a day of back-and-forth fighting. On the Plank Road, Hancock began the day by pushing Hill's Confederates back to the Tapp field. A counterattack by Longstreet by way of the unfinished railroad in turn sent Hancock's men running for their lives to the Brock Road. Lee assaulted them there late in the afternoon, but the attack failed miserably. More successful was Gordon's attack on the Union right late in the day.

GPS N 38° .171948 W 77° .433601

STOP 10: TAPP FIELD

This field was farmed by Catharine Tapp, a 59-year-old widow who shared her small log cabin with six others. Confederate troops marched by the field on May 5, on their way toward the Brock Road intersection. With them rode Robert E. Lee, who pulled aside to confer with Gens. A. P. Hill and Jeb Stuart in this field. As they were talking, a body of Union infantry emerged from the woods

Lee tried to lead the Texas Brigade into battle, but they would not let him. "Lee to the rear!" they cried. (FSNMP)

Three monuments mark the area where Lee met the Texans, including this granite marker installed in 1903 by James Power Smith, a former member of Stonewall Jackson's staff; a tablet of pink granite erected by the state of Texas for the Civil War centennial; and a nondescript quartz bolder placed by veterans (visible in the background). (DP)

just a short distance away. Surprised as much by the generals as the generals were by them, the Union soldiers disappeared into the woods as quickly as they came, thus missing a chance to bag three of the Confederacy's top leaders.

The following day, Union troops routed Hill's Confederates near the Brock Road and drove them back to this field in disorder. A dozen Confederate cannon of Lt. Col. William T. Poague's artillery battalion momentarily checked the Union pursuit here until Lt. Gen. James Longstreet's Corps arrived a few minutes later. Leading Longstreet's column was the famous Texas Brigade. "At this critical juncture," remembered Poague, "Gregg's Texans came in line of battle at a swinging gait from the rear of our position. They passed through our guns, their right near the road. General Lee was riding close behind them." As the Texans started toward the enemy, located at the edge of the woods ahead of you, Lee accompanied them, intent on leading them in the charge. "Soon the Texans began to call to General Lee to go back," wrote Poague, "and as he seemed not to heed they became clamorous, insisting that if he did not go back they would not go forward. Several members of his staff were riding behind the general and finally one of them moved to his side and touching him on the arm said something which

I could not hear. Then, turning Traveller about, he rode quietly to the rear of our line of guns, amid the cheers of the artillerymen." With Lee out of danger, the Texans continued forward. Five hundred of the brigade's 800 men fell in the charge.

The Texas Brigade's attack gave Longstreet the time he needed to deploy the rest of his corps into a line of battle near this point. Once in line, the Confederates slowly but steadily pushed Hancock's men back toward the Brock Road. But they could do no more, and by late morning a stalemate ensued. It would take a bold stroke to break the impasse.

Before leaving this stop, you may wish to explore the half-mile-long walking trail. When you are ready to leave, turn left out of the parking lot and drive two-thirds of a mile to the Wadsworth Monument pull-off, located on the left side of the road.

GPS N 38° .174264 W 77° .430493

STOP 11: WADSWORTH MONUMENT

James S. Wadsworth was having a bad week. The 57-year-old New York general had led his division into the Wilderness hoping for victory. Instead, he had experienced humiliating defeat. On May 5, Ewell's Confederates had routed Wadsworth's troops near the Orange Turnpike. The following day, after some initial success, Longstreet's Corps had routed his troops again, this time along the Orange Plank Road. The experience left Wadsworth despondent. Talking to a member of his staff during a lull in the fight, he admitted feeling "completely exhausted and worn out" and suggested "that he was unfit to command, and felt that he ought, in justice to himself and his men, to turn the command of the division over to Gen. Cutler."

Brig. Gen. James S. Wadsworth was the highest-ranking officer killed in the Wilderness. (LOC)

Minutes later, a roar of musketry erupted south of the road. Stopped by the Federals here along the Plank Road, Longstreet had dispatched four brigades down an unfinished railroad bed to turn the Union army's left flank, in the woods half a mile to your right. Coming shortly before noon, Longstreet's attack routed Hancock's force and sent it fleeing toward the Brock Road.

Wadsworth was near here when the thunderbolt struck. As he tried to wheel a couple of regiments left to meet the threat, his horse panicked and galloped

Wadsworth's division in the Wilderness (FSNMP)

toward the enemy line. Wadsworth reined in the animal just short of the Confederates. Ignoring calls to surrender, he spurred his horse back toward Union lines. He never made it. As Wadsworth turned, a line of rifles opened fire, and he fell mortally wounded with a bullet to the brain.

Surgeon J. Boylston Adams of the 56th Massachusetts too had been wounded in the battle. As he lay unconscious, Confederate soldiers had carried him to a field hospital in the rear. Later, when he came to, he found himself lying in a tent beside another officer. "He was rather tall," Adams noted, "an eminently handsome man of commanding presence, but showing gentle breeding." The officer had a pulse and was breathing but his eyes showed no reaction to light. "His noble features were calm and natural, except that his mouth was drawn down at the left side. His right arm was evidently paralyzed, which indicated that the injury was to the left brain. Examining further, I found that a musket ball had entered the top of his head a little to the left of the median line. In his left hand, which lay quietly upon the breast of his buttoned coat, he held a scrap of paper, on which was written, 'Gen. James W. Wadsworth.'"

Despite efforts by Confederate surgeons to save his life, Wadsworth did not recover.

Ease back onto the road, being careful of traffic. Drive just one-quarter mile then turn right into the small parking area on the right side of the road. When you get out of your vehicle, stand so that the road is on your left.

GPS N 38° .175266 W 77° .425237

STOP 12: LONGSTREET'S WOUNDING

With Wadsworth's fall, resistance on the Plank Road collapsed. Union troops fled eastward to the Brock Road, where General Hancock personally rallied them and set them to work digging in.

On the heels of the defeated Union army came Longstreet. Exuberant over the success of the flank attack, he led his troops forward down the Plank Road in pursuit of the retreating foe with a small group of staff officers and couriers at his side. Up from the rear road came 29-year-old Brig. Gen. Micah Jenkins, who commanded a South Carolina brigade nearby. Jenkins's face was radiant with joy. Grasping Longstreet's hand, he congratulated his chief on the success of the attack, and then, turning to his brigade, he shouted: "Why do you not cheer, men?" The men hardly had time to respond when a volley, fired by the flanking party, exploded from these woods. One of the bullets embedded itself in Jenkins's brain; another struck Longstreet near the base of the neck. Staff officers helped Longstreet from his saddle, laying him down beside the road until an ambulance arrived to carry him to the rear. Although surgeons initially considered the wound to be fatal, the general recovered and returned to the army that fall. The same could not be said of Jenkins. Like Wadsworth, he died at a Confederate field hospital a few hours later.

Longstreet, Wadsworth, and Jenkins were among the 30,000 casualties suffered by the Union and Confederate armies in the Wilderness. When the medical department proved incapable of handling the large numbers of wounded soldiers, men like Quartermaster Orsel C. Brown of the 44th New York Volunteers were pressed into service. "While the

Lt. Gen. James Longstreet had been the best man at Ulysses Grant's wedding to Julia Dent in 1848. (LOC)

General James Longstreet was shot by "friendly fire" in the Wilderness, one year to the week after Stonewall Jackson fell under similar circumstances just a few miles away. (FSNMP)

Brig. Gen. Micah Jenkins died in the same volley that wounded Longstreet. (FSNMP)

sufferer lay upon the amputating table I administered the chloroform," he explained, "and then would witness whatever operation it was necessary to perform doing what I could to assist the surgeons. Legs, arms and fingers were taken off and broken ones set, balls were taken from all parts of the body and rapidly were the wounds dressed and the patient borne to his couch upon the ground. We cared for them the best we could but oh! how they suffered."

The Confederate wounded made their way back to Orange, Virginia, thence to cities like Lynchburg or Richmond, while wounded Union soldiers were sent back through Fredericksburg to Aquia Landing, where they boarded ships for hospitals in the North.

The dead remained on the battlefield, at least for a time. In 1865, the United States government created two cemeteries for the Union dead in the Wilderness, one at Saunders field and the other here beside the Orange Plank Road. Their remains were later transferred to the national cemetery in Fredericksburg. Southern citizens buried their dead at a Confederate cemetery in town.

Continue down the Orange Plank Road one-third mile to the Brock Road, parking in the same lot as before. This time face west toward the Confederates. The Brock Road should be behind you and the Plank Road should be on your right.

GPS N 38° .180289 W 77° .423438

STOP 13: THE BROCK ROAD/PLANK ROAD INTERSECTION

After being routed by Longstreet, Union troops fell back to the Brock Road and hastily constructed earthworks. (FSNMP)

Following Longstreet's May 6 flank attack, Union soldiers fell back here to the Brock Road, where General Hancock reorganized them and put them to work digging entrenchments, faint remnants of which can still be seen between the parking lot and the Brock Road. Artillerist Charles Brockway watched his comrades as they went to work. "With instinctive haste the men began constructing breastworks, using for that purpose old logs, planks torn from the road, in fact, anything that would stop a bullet," he wrote. "The pioneer corps was busily engaged in slashing trees in front of the works, either to give play to some few guns which were in position, or to impede the enemy should they charge. No noise betokened the presence of our foes, yet 'we felt in our bones' that they were not far off."

Fortunately for Hancock, Longstreet's wounding had hampered the Confederate pursuit. It was 4 p.m. before Lee was able to marshal Longstreet's forces for a final push against the Brock Road, behind you. By then, Hancock's men had recovered from their panic and resolutely awaited the attack from the protection of three parallel lines of earthworks bordering the road. Here, at the intersection, Union troops mowed down the Confederates as they emerged from the woods into a narrow clearing made by the pioneer corps, but 200 yards to your left it was a different matter. There, the Union logworks had

taken fire, forcing Union defenders to fall back. Soldiers of Jenkins's brigade exploited the gap, planting their battle flags on the burning works. For a moment, it looked as though Lee's men might triumph, but just then, through the smoke, Brig. Gen. Samuel Carroll's brigade appeared and with a wild hurrah swept into the road and reclaimed the lost works. Defeated, Lee's men drifted back into the deep woods and began throwing up earthworks of their own back at the Tapp field.

When their logworks caught fire (top), Confederates briefly broke through (above), but a Federal counterattack led by Brig. Gen. Samuel Carroll (below) succeeded in stopping them and recapturing the Brock Road. (FSNMP)

With Lee's army firmly entrenched in his front, Grant saw no chance for a successful attack. On May 7, he determined to leave the Wilderness. "My object in moving to Spottsyvlania was two-fold," he later explained, "first, I did not want Lee to get back to Richmond in time to attempt to crush Butler before I could get there; second, I wanted to get between his army and Richmond if possible; and, if not, to draw him into the open field."

After nightfall, the Army of the Potomac quietly filed out of its trenches and started south toward Spotsylvania Court House, the next stop on the road to Richmond. After two days of savage

Despite appallingly high losses in the Wilderness, Union troops cheered Grant when he made the choice to maneuver around Lee's army. (FSNMP)

fighting, most Union soldiers expected Grant to retreat. But to their surprise, the army continued south. "Gen Grant does not seem inclined to retreat because the army under his direction gets temporarily repulsed," mused one New York soldier. "Our former experiences led us to believe that we would necessarily recross the Rapidan some days since. That this time dont seem to be in the programme." Heartened by their new commander's resolve, Union soldiers spontaneously cheered Grant as he passed. Lieutenant Colonel Horace Porter of Grant's staff recalled that "Soldiers weary and sleepy after their long battle, with stiffened limbs and smarting wounds, now sprang to their feet, forgetful of their pains, and rushed forward to the roadside. Wild cheers echoed through the forest, and glad shouts of triumph rent the air. Men swung their hats, tossed up their arms, and pressed forward to within touch of their chief, clapping their hands, and speaking to him with the familiarity of comrades. Pine-knots and leaves were set on fire, and lighted the scene with their weird, flickering glare. The night march had become a triumphal procession for the new commander."

Meanwhile, less than two miles away, Southern troops too were raising their voices in triumph. A soldier in McGowan's brigade witnessed the vocal demonstration.

We were moved a few hundred yards to the right, and

there rested until morning. While we were closing up here, a pace at a time, the grandest vocal exhibition took place that I have ever heard. Far up on the right of the Confederate line a shout was raised. Gradually it was taken up and passed down, until it reached us. We lifted it, as our turn came, and handed it to the left, where it went echoing to the remotest corner of Ewell's corps. This was done once with powerful effect . . . . Again the shout arose on the right—again it rushed down upon us from a distance of perhaps two miles—again we caught it and flung it joyously to the left, where it only ceased when the last post had huzzahed. And yet a third time this mighty wave of sound rang along the Confederate lines. The effect was beyond expression. It seemed to fill every heart with new life, to inspire every nerve with might never known before. Men seemed fairly convulsed with the fierce enthusiasm; and I believe that if at that instant the advance of the whole army upon Grant could have been ordered, we should have swept it into the very Rappahannock.

Skeletons littered the woods in the months following the battle. (FSNMP)

Both sides claimed victory in the Wilderness, and in a sense both were right. In terms of casualties, the Army of Northern Virginia had won a resounding victory. In two days of combat, it had inflicted some 20,000 casualties on the Union army while sustaining little more than half that number itself. On the other hand, the Army of the Potomac could claim success in that it had safely crossed the Rapidan River and was continuing its march to Richmond. Corporal John Haley of the 17th Maine got it just about right when, casting his eyes upon the dark woods now "filled with dead and wounded from both sides," he concluded that "Neither side appears to have gained much from this struggle in the Wilderness."

The battle of the Wilderness was not only among the most deadly but, with the fires in the dense forest, also the most horrific in American history. But ahead lay an even more horrific and more deadly struggle: the battle of Spotsylvania Court House.

In 1865, the United States Government created two cemeteries in the Wilderness, one of which stood beside the Orange Plank Road. (FSNMP)

Opposite: Confederate artillery in Tapp Field (DP)

Spotsylvania Court House

CHAPTER TWO

MAY 8-22, 1864

The battle of the Wilderness marked the first of many battles that would ultimately lead to the surrender of Lee's army at Appomattox. The bloodiest and most frightful of these was Spotsylvania Court House. Fought over a period of two weeks, much of it amid pouring rain, the battle featured episodes of fighting so brutal, so savage, that witnesses were at a loss to describe it. Phrases like "piles of corpses" and "trenches crimson with blood," often used in hyperbole, were all too literal here. Wrote one participant, "It seemed as though instead of being human we were turned into fiends and brutes, seeking to kill all in our way."

To begin your tour of Spotsylvania, begin at the Brock Road/ Plank Road intersection on the Wilderness battlefield. From that intersection, drive south on the Brock Road (Route 613) a distance of 1.2 miles to a gravel road now known as Jackson Trail West. Stop in front of the historical signs.

GPS N 38° .171748 W 77° .414900

STOP 1: JACKSON TRAIL WEST

This gravel road, now known as Jackson Trail West, is named after "Stonewall" Jackson, who, in 1863, had used the road to outflank the Union army at Chancellorsville. One year later, Lt. Gen. Ulysses S. Grant accidentally turned onto this road as he rode toward Spotsylvania Court House, in the wake of Maj. Gen. Philip Sheridan's cavalry.

A soldier from the 15th New Jersey stands vigil over Spotsylvania's Bloody Angle. (DP)

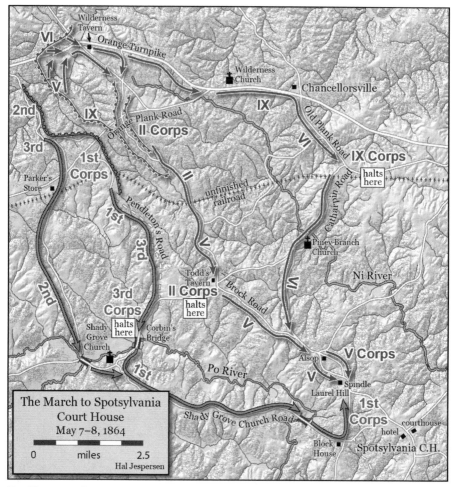

THE MARCH TO SPOTSYLVANIA COURT HOUSE—Confederates carved their own road out of the Wilderness, then took a roundabout march to beat Federals to Spotsylvania Court House. Federals, stymied by Confederate cavalry delaying actions along the Brock Road, were further hampered by the size of their own army as it tried to move over narrow, unpaved roads.

It was a mistake that could have had disastrous consequences. As Grant himself explained: "Meade and I rode in advance. We had passed but a little way beyond our left when the road forked. We looked to see, if we could, which road Sheridan had taken with his cavalry during the day. It seemed to be the right-hand one, and accordingly we took it." A little ways beyond, Grant's chief engineer, Col. Cyrus B. Comstock, rode past the party alone and at a gallop. "In a few minutes," wrote Grant, "he returned and reported that Lee was moving, and that the road we were on would bring us into his lines in a short distance. We returned to the forks of the road, left a man to indicate the right road to the head of Warren's column when it should come up, and continued our journey to Todd's Tavern, where we arrived after midnight."

Grant consented to return to this road fork only after his guide was unable to find a shortcut to the Brock Road through the woods. As Lt. Col. Horace Porter of Grant's staff explained, the general had a "marked aversion to turning back, which amounted almost to a superstition."

The march to Spotsylvania Court House (FSNMP)

Soldiers in both armies long remembered the night march to Spotsylvania Court House. "Tedious beyond all power to describe was the experience of that night," wrote one Union soldier. "The march was slow, with many halts. At every stop the men would fall asleep; it was almost impossible to keep awake while traveling, and they were roused with extreme difficulty in many cases. The extreme nervous strain had made sad havoc with self-control of man, and the slightest unexpected noise seemed almost to create a panic . . . ."

Everyone's nerves were on edge. Thomas Marbaker of the 11th New Jersey experienced firsthand the imagined terrors of that night. "The stillness of the night, the gloom of the forest, so deep as to be almost shadowless, making the forms of comrades only a pace or two distant look like dim silhouettes against a darker background; clumps of bushes, stumps and fallen limbs took weird and threatening shapes; imagination played fantastic tricks, and fallen logs became lurking foes and the harmless murmur of each gentle breeze the voice of waiting enemies, and as we moved slowly forward through the gloom our feet would come in contact with some yielding substance, and, reaching down, our hands perhaps would fall upon the clammy face of a corpse, for the woods was filled with death's ghastly trophy."

The Army of the Potomac's night march to Spotsylvania Court House was as slow as it was stressful. Every few hundred yards, the soldiers had to stop to wait for the troops ahead of them to move on. A Union officer blamed a wet spot just south of here for at least part of the delay. "About two miles out on the Brock road," he wrote, "beyond where our left rested, we found . . . a very large mud hole, taking up the whole width of the road. Across one side was a fallen tree forming a foot bridge. From the tracks it was evident that this mud hole had been a very serious obstacle as the men had gone everywhere except through it and . . . this accounted for the delay." The delay occasioned by the mud hole, though minor, would have serious ramifications in the day ahead.

Carefully pull back onto the Brock Road (Route 613) and continue south for 3.6 miles and park at the small lot you find on the right.

GPS N 38° .145105 W 77° .400730

STOP 2: TODD'S TAVERN

Todd's Tavern (FSNMP)

Here, at the intersection of the Brock and Catharpin roads, stood a rustic hostelry known as Todd's Tavern. Built by the Todd family prior to 1835, by the Civil War the one-and-one-half-story ramshackle frame structure was the property of Charles Bradshaw. A Union soldier who visited the unpretentious structure declared that it had "no merits, architectural or otherwise, to warrant its becoming a conspicuous landmark of the campaign."

General Fitzhugh Lee's Confederate cavalry held this intersection until forced back toward Spotsylvania Court House by Phil Sheridan's Union horsemen on May 7. Sheridan had orders to clear the road all the way to Spotsylvania Court House, but when Grant and Meade arrived here about midnight on May 8, they learned that Lee's horsemen continued to block the Brock Road farther south. Meade angrily roused Sheridan's horsemen from their slumbers around the tavern and ordered them to clear the road. He and Grant then took up quarters inside the building, where they grabbed a few hours' sleep before continuing toward Spotsylvania.

A few hours later, Maj. Gen. Winfield S. Hancock's II Corps arrived at Todd's Tavern. Fearing that Robert E. Lee might strike at his army by way of the Catharpin Road, to your right, Meade

Brig. Gen. Fitzhugh Lee (LOC)

The army marching past Todd's Tavern (FSNMP)

ordered the II Corps to halt at Todd's Tavern and dig in. Hancock remained here throughout May 8, anxiously awaiting an attack that never came. On May 9, he continued south, joining the rest of the army near Spotsylvania Court House.

Continue south on the Brock Road (Route 613) 2.2 miles to the junction of Piney Branch Road (Route 624). Note the junction but do not stop there. Instead, continue 0.6 mile farther to Gordon Road (Route 612), on your left. At the Gordon Road junction is Goshen Baptist Church. Park in the church lot and face south so that Gordon Road is in front of you.

GPS N 38° .133532 W 77° .373482

STOP 3: BROCK ROAD FORK

Forced to relinquish Todd's Tavern on May 7, Fitzhugh Lee's Confederates fell back down the Brock Road to Piney Branch Road, which you passed half a mile up the road. Here they erected a barricade across the Brock Road in an effort to block the Union army's advance toward Spotsylvania Court House. Late in the afternoon, Union horsemen attacked Lee down both the Brock and the Piney Branch roads. Lee put up a stubborn fight, but he ultimately had to relinquish the ground and fall back. Rather than pursue the Confederates to Spotsylvania, thus clearing the way for the infantry, Sheridan's cavalry fell back to Todd's Tavern and went into camp, allowing Lee to reoccupy the Piney Branch Road works.

The Brock Road (FSNMP)

When Sheridan's cavalry resumed its advance toward Spotsylvania at midnight, May 8, Fitz Lee's

The Federal infantry's advance to Spotsylvania was slower than expected because of delays caused by Confederate cavalry and the poor performance of Sheridan's horsemen. (LOC)

division again stood in its way. For the second time in 12 hours, the Union horsemen attacked Lee there. The Confederates gamely stood their ground but had to fall back when Brig. Gen. John C. Robinson's Union infantry division was brought forward. From that point on, Robinson's division would lead the Union advance on Spotsylvania Court House.

At this point, the Brock Road divided into two roads that paralleled one another for approximately one mile. The modern Brock Road follows the right-hand fork of the road. Ahead of you is the left-hand fork, now a private road called Atwood Lane. Between the two forks stood the Alsop farm. In this clearing, Maj. James Breathed unlimbered two cannons in an effort to check the Union army's advance. As Robinson's men approached, one of the guns moved off. Breathed held his ground with the other, hoping to get off one more shot at the Federals before retiring to safety. He nearly tarried too long. Pressing forward, Robinson's men leveled a volley at Breathed, killing several of his horses. "Surrender that gun, you rebel scoundrel," one Northern soldier cried. Instead, the 23-year-old Confederate officer cut the traces of the fallen horses and, leaping on one of the remaining animals, pulled the gun away amid a hail of musketry. One of the Union soldiers who confronted Breathed that day wrote that it was the greatest display of bravery he witnessed during the war.

Brig. Gen. John C. Robinson's infantry division engaged in a running cat-and-mouse battle with the Confederate cavalry blocking the road to Spotsylvania Court House. (FSNMP)

Major General Gouverneur K. Warren accompanied Robinson's division. As Robinson's men drove Fitz Lee's cavalry from one position to the next, Warren's optimism grew. "The opposition to us amounts to nothing as yet," he wrote Meade at 8 a.m.; "we are advancing steadily . . . . [I]f there is nothing but cavalry, we shall scarcely halt."

Return to the Brock Road (Route 613) and turn left. Drive one mile and turn left into Spotsylvania battlefield. Just inside the entrance, on the left, is a National Park Service shelter with exhibit panels describing the battle. Park there and walk back to the Brock Road. Near the road is a large granite monument dedicated to Maj. Gen. John Sedgwick. Visible across the Brock Road is the Spindle house clearing, later known as Laurel Hill, where the opening engagement of the battle occurred. Stand facing the field.

GPS N 38° .130423 W 77° .365247

STOP 4: LAUREL HILL

It was approaching 9 a.m., May 8, when Brig. Gen. John Robinson's division reached this point, the Spindle farm, less than two miles from Spotsylvania Court House. The temperature had started to rise, and by the time Robinson's men reached the Spindle farm clearing they were not only tired but hot. Private James L. Bowen of the 37th Massachusetts remembered that the "heat had become intense and enervating, the roads were dry as tinder and the dust rose in stifling clouds, which hung with torturing persistency close to the earth choking the lungs, the throat, the eyes and settling in disgusting quantity upon the sweaty flesh wherever it could penetrate."

Laurel Hill (FSNMP)

Utterly worn out by the running pursuit of the enemy, Robinson's men collapsed to the ground, gasping for breath. But there was no time to rest. A few hundred yards away, on the far side of the clearing, Fitzhugh Lee's cavalrymen were hastily piling up fence rails in a last-ditch effort to defend Spotsylvania Court House. Placing himself at the head of the Maryland Brigade, Robinson led his division forward. Brigadier General Charles Griffin's division advanced simultaneously on his right. When within 50 yards of the Confederate line, a rifle ball shattered Robinson's knee. Two leaders of the Maryland Brigade fell in quick succession.

Too late the Federals realized that they confronted not only Fitz Lee's cavalry, but Maj. Gen. Richard H. Anderson's infantry, too. One day earlier, Gen. Robert E. Lee had promoted

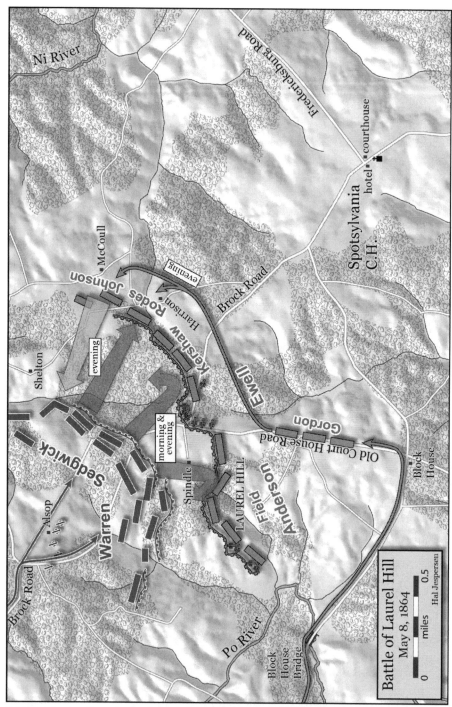

Battle of Laurel Hill
May 8, 1864
Hal Jespersen

BATTLE OF LAUREL HILL—As Confederate infantry arrived on the field, they funneled into place just in time to bottleneck the Federals, who made piecemeal attacks up the Brock Road and across Spindle field. The arrival of reinforcements later in the day did nothing to break the impasse, although Federals did briefly penetrate the Southern works.

Anderson to command of the army's First Corps following Lt. Gen. James Longstreet's wounding in the Wilderness. The previous night, while Warren was slowly advancing toward Spotsylvania on the Brock Road, Anderson was making his way toward the town by a parallel route to the west. Advancing at a run, the head of Anderson's column reached Laurel Hill just minutes ahead of Warren. When Robinson's division charged across the field that morning, they were met not by the pop of cavalry carbines but by the roar of infantry rifles. By the slightest of margins, the Confederates had won the race to Spotsylvania.

Maj. Gen. Richard Anderson commanded the Confederate First Corps following the wounding of James Longstreet in the Wilderness on May 6. (LOC)

Anderson's men immediately began to entrench. "A bunch of leaves, a tuft of grass, loose dirt, rotten trees, anything that had the semblance of firmness went into the little trenches that we made and laid down in. We dug dirt with tin pans, tin cups, knives, rails, anything," wrote William Abernathy of the 17th Mississippi. As the remaining divisions of his corps reached the field, Warren threw them into action in a series of bloody, piecemeal assaults that failed to dent the Confederate line. By noon, he had given up the notion of capturing Spotsylvania and was thinking defensively. In a dispatch to Meade, he wrote: "My position is good enough if I am not attacked in some unprepared point on my flanks. I incline to think, though, that if I let the enemy alone he will me. I cannot gain Spotsylvania Court-House with what force I have."

As additional troops reached the battlefield, the two armies extended their lines and entrenched. "By the middle of the afternoon," wrote South Carolinian John Coxe, "thousands of troops of both sides having arrived, we took position, began to build breastworks, and settled down to a death

The Union V Corps could not break through Confederate defenses. (FSNMP)

Maj. Gen. John Sedgwick was the highest-ranking Union officer killed during the war. Sedgwick died when a bullet fired by a Confederate sharpshooter using a special Whitworth rifle outfitted with a telescopic sight struck him just below the eye. Confederates had been peppering the area all morning, wounding, among others, Brig. Gen. William H. Morris. (FSNMP)

struggle. Bullets and shrieking shells filled the air, and one had to be very careful or stand a good chance of being picked off."

Here, on the north side of the field, Sedgwick's VI Corps filed into trenches beside Warren's men. Sedgwick made his headquarters just behind the line. At the intersection stood a section of artillery. When he noticed that one of his regiments was blocking the guns, Sedgwick walked over here to straighten things out. With him was his 25-year-old adjutant, Lt. Col. Martin T. McMahon. Earlier in the day, McMahon had warned Sedgwick to avoid the intersection, as Confederate sharpshooters had been active that morning. In their eagerness to straighten out the line, however, both officers forgot the danger. McMahon described what happened next.

I gave the necessary order to move the troops to the right, and as they rose to execute the movement the enemy opened a sprinkling fire, partly from sharp-shooters. As the bullet whistled by, some of the men dodged. The general said laughingly, "What! what! men, dodging this way for single bullets! What will you do when they open fire along the whole line? I am ashamed of you. They couldn't hit an elephant at this distance." A few seconds after, a man who had been separated from his regiment passed directly in front of the general, and at the same moment a sharpshooter's bullet passed with a long shrill whistle very close, and the soldier, who was then just in front of the general, dodged to the ground. The general touched him gently with his foot, and said, "Why, my man, I am ashamed of you, dodging that way," and repeated the remark, "They couldn't hit an elephant at this distance." The man rose and saluted, and said good-naturedly, "General, I dodged a shell once, and if I hadn't, it would have taken my head off. I believe in dodging." The general laughed and replied, "All right, my man; go to your place."

Sedgwick was so beloved by his men that they called him "Uncle John." (LOC)

For a third time the same shrill whistle, closing with a dull, heavy stroke, interrupted our talk, when, as I was about to resume, the general's face turned slowly to me, the blood spurting from his left cheek under the eye in a steady stream. He fell in my direction; I was so close to him that my effort to support him failed, and I fell with him.

Blood bubbled from the wound like water from a fountain. Within minutes, Sedgwick was dead. Grant received the news with stunned incredulity, twice asking the messenger, "Is he really dead?" He later remarked that Sedgwick's loss to the army was greater than that of a whole division of troops.

The fighting at Laurel Hill continued on and off for several more days. On May 10 and again on May 12, Warren's troops surged across the Spindle fields to attack Anderson's entrenched position. With each attack, the number of Union casualties grew. Realizing that Laurel Hill could not be taken, Grant set his sights on a more promising target: a huge outward bulge in the center of the Confederate line known as the Muleshoe Salient.

Spotsylvania battlefield has seven miles of hiking trails. Printed guides in a box adjacent to the exhibit shelter show the location of these trails. Get back in your vehicle now and turn left onto the park tour road. Drive one-half mile to a pullout for Upton's Road, on the right.

GPS N 38° .132333 W 77° .362075

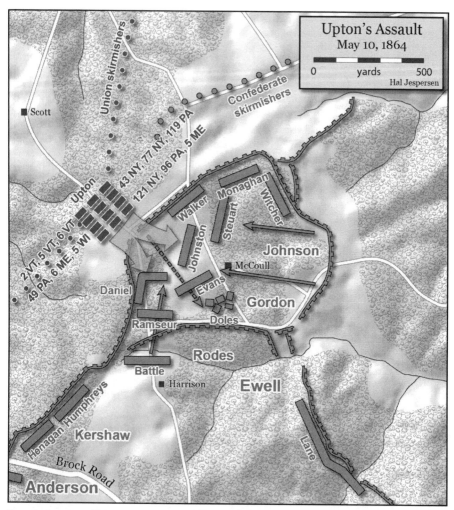

UPTON'S ASSAULT—After organizing his attack force into a column three regiments wide and four regiments deep, Upton charged them across 200 yards of open field to strike a hammer-like blow against Confederates under George Doles. Upton's first row breached the Confederate line; the second row widened the gap; the third pushed into the breach; the fourth served as reserve. As Confederate reinforcements rushed to the scene, Upton's unsupported men were forced to fall back.

STOP 5: UPTON'S ROAD

Grant's first impulse upon reaching Spotsylvania was to defeat Lee by turning his flanks. When both the left and right ends of the Confederate line appeared strong, however, Grant mistakenly concluded that the line must be weak in the center—either at Laurel Hill or farther to the left, near the McCoull house. On May 10, he ordered a general assault on the Confederate line.

Twenty-five-year-old Col. Emory Upton

spearheaded the assault. Upton's skirmishers advanced left to right through these woods, pushing Lee's pickets back to their works, one-quarter mile to your right. Once in possession of these woods, Upton led 5,000 men down this woods road to a point within 300 yards of the Confederate line. There, in the depths of the woods, he formed them into a column of attack, four lines deep. Corporal Clinton Beckwith of the 121st New York was in the first line. "We were ordered to fix bayonets, to load and cap our guns and to charge at a right shoulder shift arms. No man was to stop and succor or assist a wounded comrade. We must go as far as possible, and when we broke their line, face to our right, advance and fire lengthwise of their line. Colonel Upton was with our regiment and rode on our right. He instructed us not to fire a shot, cheer or yell, until we struck their works."

The attack began around 6 p.m., preceded by an artillery bombardment. After a few minutes the artillery ceased its fire and Upton's men moved forward. "I felt my gorge rise," remembered Beckwith, "and my stomach and intestines shrink together in a knot, and a thousand things rushed through my mind. I fully realized the terrible peril I was to encounter . . . . I looked about in the faces of the boys around me, and they told the tale of expected death. Pulling my cap down over my eyes, I stepped out . . . ." When they reached the field, the Union soldiers cheered and broke into a run. The Confederates responded with a volley, and men began to fall.

Upton led his men through the woods along a road that still exists as a trail that visitors can hike. (DP)

A few yards in front of the Confederate line stood a line of felled trees, known as abatis. As the Federals paused to make their way through the slashings, the Confederates poured in a second volley. In front was a Union officer. Leaping on top of the Confederate works, he shouted, "Come on, men," and then pitched forward dead. By then, Beckwith and others too were cascading over the works. "As I got on top some Rebs jumped up from their side and began to run back," he recalled. "Some were lunging at our men with their bayonets and a few had their guns clubbed . . . . I fired into

Colonel Emory Upton viewed war as a science and was its most avid student. During the war he served in all three fighting branches of the army: the infantry, cavalry, and artillery. After the war, he went on to become one of the most influential tacticians in U.S. army history. (LOC)

In order to delay and break up enemy assaults, the Confederates strengthened their defenses by placing rows of sharpened branches in front of their line. (FSNMP)

them, jumped down into the pits and moved out toward them . . . . While moving as ordered, some Rebel troops came up and fired a volley into us. We got on the other side of the rifle pits and began firing at them and checked their advance. It was now duskish and it seemed as though the firing on our front and to our right became heavier, and the whistle of balls seemed to come from all directions and was incessant . . . ."

Once over the works, Upton's men engaged the Confederates in deadly hand-to-hand combat. "The enemy sitting in their pits with pieces upright, loaded, and with bayonets fixed, ready to impale the first who should leap over, absolutely refused to yield the ground," wrote Upton. "The first of our men who tried to surmount the works fell pierced through the head by musket-balls. Others, seeing the fate of their comrades, held their pieces at arms length and fired downward, while others, poising their pieces vertically, hurled them down upon their enemy, pinning them to the ground . . . . The struggle lasted but a few seconds. Numbers prevailed, and, like a resistless wave, the column poured over the works, quickly putting *hors de combat* those who resisted, and sending to the rear those who surrendered."

The point attacked by Upton was known as Doles's Salient after the Confederate officer whose troops defended it. We'll pick up the story of Upton's attack there. To reach Doles's Salient, you can walk the Upton's Road trail for 350 yards or you can drive to the site by following the park tour road 0.3 mile to a sharp right-hand turn (Anderson Drive) and then proceeding 0.2 mile farther to a pullout with two signs on the right.

GPS N 38° .131626 W 77° .361228

STOP 6: DOLES'S SALIENT

The gentle mounds on your right, now covered by brush, are all that remain of a six-mile-long line of earthworks that protected Lee's men. The line ran from the Po River, on Lee's left, to a point beyond Spotsylvania Court House, on his right. Brigadier General James A. Walker, who commanded the Stonewall Brigade, remembered constructing the works in this vicinity on the night of May 8. "The greater part of the line of the division was along the outer edge . . . of a body of fine oak timber," he recalled. "As soon as night put an end to the combat, axes, picks and shovels were sent for, and along the whole line through the night the men worked like beavers, and the crash of falling trees, the ring of axes, and the sound of the spade and shovel were heard. Trees were felled and piled upon each other, and a ditch dug behind them with the earth out of it thrown against the logs. The limbs and tops of the trees cut off from the trunks were used to form abatis, by placing them in front of the breastworks with the sharpened points towards the enemy . . . ." The Confederates continued to improve these works over the next four days, turning them into one of the best lines of temporary earthworks that Walker ever saw. "It was apparently impregnable," he wrote. "Just behind the intrenched line of infantry, artillery was placed at the

Brigadier General George Doles narrowly escaped capture on May 10 only to die less than one month later at Bethesda Church. (LOC)

Upton's men herded 1,000 of Doles's men back to Union lines—so many that the men of Smith's battery mistook the movement as a Confederate counterattack. (FSNMP)

most eligible points, to sweep the approaching enemy with shot and shell and cannister."

Although the works seemed impregnable, the Army of the Potomac successfully breached them on two different occasions: on May 10 during Upton's assault, and again on May 12 at the East Angle. Upton's assault struck the Confederate works here at an outward bend in the line known as Doles's Salient. Although Upton's attack achieved initial success and garnered more than 1,000 Confederate prisoners, the Union colonel was not properly supported and, as night fell, and he reluctantly gave orders to withdraw. His success here, however, prompted Grant to attack the Muleshoe Salient two days later.

Just 100 yards ahead on the park tour road are two cannons representing Capt. Benjamin H. Smith's battery of the Richmond Howitzers battalion. Stroll over to the guns and face the open field.

GPS N 38° .131266 W 77° .361290

STOP 7: SMITH'S BATTERY

Brigadier General George P. Doles's Georgia brigade defended this part of the Muleshoe Salient. Supporting it were four guns of the Richmond Howitzers, commanded by Capt. Benjamin H.

Smith. Sergeant William White was an artillerist in the battery. Around 6 p.m., he and his comrades here endured shelling from three Union batteries—18 guns—that were less than a mile away. Forty minutes later, the Union guns fell silent and Upton's men started forward.

Upton's men overran Smith's battery on May 10, but Confederates ultimately recaptured the guns. (DP)

"Make ready, boys—that are charging!" came the cry. A moment later, Upton's men spilled over the works to your right, scooping up more than 1,000 prisoners, whom they quickly herded to the rear.

Once over the works, some of Upton's men wheeled in this direction, attacking Smith's battery from the right and rear. Sergeant White described what happened next: "The fourth detachment fights its gun until the first gun is captured, the second gun is captured, the third gun is captured, and its own limber-chest [is] captured! . . . Our support was breaking on all sides—on our right and rear the enemy were pouring in upon us in a perfect avalanche. And now comes over us a feeling of sickening horror—not the fear of death, for, so help us God, we thought not of dying, but we thought of the shame in leaving our battery to be captured by the enemy, and that, too, almost without a struggle." White and several other men scrambled over the earthworks in front of the guns in order to protect themselves and then ran left along the outside of the works to safety. "Everything was in the direst confusion," remembered White, "all company organization was entirely broken up. Our men, being ordered to take care of themselves, got out of the enemy's way as best they could, scarcely any two of them going together . . . ."

Although the suddenness of Upton's attack momentarily threw the Confederates into confusion, they quickly recovered. At dark, they expelled Upton's troops from the works and recaptured Smith's guns, which they turned on the retreating foe. Upton's attack had failed because it lacked proper support. Grant would not make the same mistake twice. When he assailed the Muleshoe Salient two days later, he committed his entire army to the attack.

If your vehicle is still at Upton's Road, drive 400 yards to the Bloody Angle parking area. If you drove to this site, make a U-turn and return to the Bloody Angle parking area, just beyond the 90-degree turn in the road. Follow the trail that leads from the parking lot out into the field. There you will see two monuments, side by side, marking the location of the Bloody Angle. Halfway between the parking lot and those monuments are two National Park Service historical signs. Stop at the signs and stand so that the tour road is behind you and the Bloody Angle is to your right-front.

GPS N 38° .132525 W 77° .360276

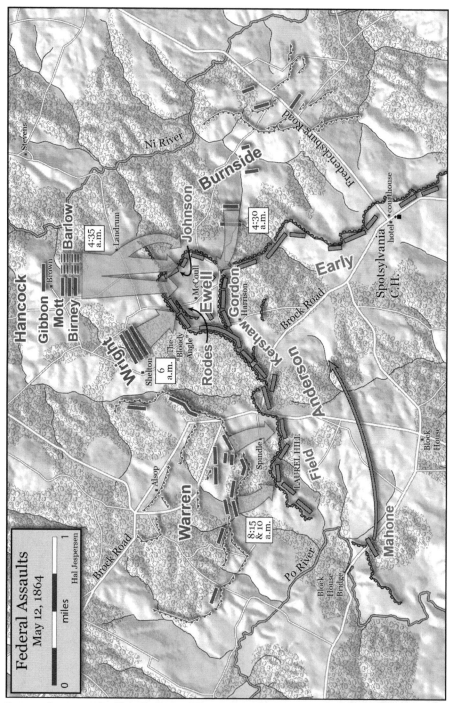

Federal Assaults
May 12, 1864

Hal Jespersen

miles

FEDERAL ASSAULTS—On May 12, Hancock's II Corps hammered the tip of the Muleshoe, with Wright's VI Corps on hand to exploit the breakthrough. On the flanks, Warren's V Corps and Burnside's IX Corps launched attacks to tie down any potential Confederate reinforcements. Downpours and darkness delayed the main attack, and Warren's supporting attack got underway even hours later than that. Burnside attacked on time but with little vigor.

STOP 8: THE BLOODY ANGLE

The fields around you comprise the bloodiest ground in all of North America. Here on May 12, 1864, Union and Confederate soldiers engaged one another in an epic struggle unmatched in American history for its stubborn ferocity and carnage. The fighting began just after dawn. Moving silently through a heavy, wet fog, the men of Hancock's II Corps, 20,000 strong, swept across the field in front of you, left to right, and cascaded over the Confederate earthworks to your right like an irresistible wave, capturing 3,000 prisoners and 20 cannon. Lee struck back hard, counterattacking with every man that he could spare. For 22 hours, the two armies battled one another face-to-face in a pouring rain. Grant fought to win; Lee to survive.

Union troops poured over the Confederate works like an irresistible wave, unhampered by the fire of Confederate artillery, which had been removed from the salient the night before. (FSNMP)

The fighting focused on a small turn in the Confederate line that became known as the "Bloody Angle." Private Andrew Long, a soldier in the 5th Virginia, was one of those engaged in the fight. "This fierce attack did not last but about an hour until General Lee sent in another division," he wrote. "From then on till midnight men slaughtered each other. Fences and logs in the breastworks became toothpicks. No sooner would a flag fall than another carrier who picked it up would be shot or bayoneted. Men were so close their heads were at the end of gun muzzles as they shot each other. When ammunition ran out or got wet they crushed each other's skulls with gun butts. They stabbed

Fighting at the Angle was fanatical, one soldier calling it "a boiling, bubbling and hissing caldron of death." (FSNMP)

Many historians consider Maj. Gen. Winfield Hancock to be the Army of the Potomac's most talented general. May 12, 1864, was his finest day. (LOC)

The combat not only ended lives, it destroyed a forest. Just inside the Angle, a 22-inch-wide oak tree toppled to the ground, felled by small-arms fire alone. The stump is now on display at the Smithsonian Institution. (FSNMP)

each other with swords. The mud of the breastworks became a mass of torn bodies as fresh troops rushed into the mouths of cannon firing double loads of canister. For nearly 20 hours we held our position."

Brigadier General Lewis A. Grant commanded a brigade of Vermont troops that fought at the Angle. He described the combat as "not only a desperate struggle but it was literally a hand-to-hand fight. Nothing but the piled up logs or breastworks separated the combatants. Our men would reach over the logs and fire into the faces of the enemy, would stab over with their bayonets; many were shot and stabbed through the crevices and holes between the logs; men mounted the works, and with muskets rapidly handed them, kept up a continuous fire until they were shot down, when others would take their place and continue the deadly work . . . . It was there that the somewhat celebrated tree was cut off by bullets, there that the bush and logs were cut to pieces and whipped into basket-stuff; . . . there that the rebel ditches and cross-sections were filled with dead men several deep."

Grant visited the Angle the following day, after the Confederates had withdrawn. "The sight was terrible and sickening, much worse than at [Antietam's] Bloody Lane. There a great many dead men were lying in the road and across the rails of the torn down fences, and out in the cornfield; but they were not piled up several deep and their flesh was not so torn and mangled as at the Angle."

It is estimated that 9,000 Union soldiers and 8,000 Confederates were casualties on May 12, most of them here at the Bloody Angle. Unable to recapture the Muleshoe, Lee ordered his troops to withdraw from the Salient after dark, conceding the field to the Federals. Private Moritz Oestreich of the 96th Pennsylvania Volunteers visited the contested ground the next day and found it almost too horrible to describe. "Thousands of dead bodies are seen and the trenches are filled with them," he wrote, "4 and 5 on top of each other, and sometimes the lowest on the bottom are wounded and alive, yet were covered with mud and smothered. Trees of 1 and 2 feet thick are shot off by musket bullets, and the wounded and dead bodies which had fallen in the first charge at the commencement of the battle were shot to pieces by the 1/2 inch and mashed.

Stacks of wood and trenches were no stronger in withstanding our brave soldiers' bullets and artillery batteries." Oestreich could not bring himself to write any more. "I have seen so much that I can't nor will put it in this book. I will seal this in my memory by myself. God, have mercy on those who started this cruel war."

We strongly encourage you to continue along this walking trail. When you are finished, get back in your vehicle and continue past the two cannons you saw earlier until you come to a fork in the road. Take the left-hand fork and park on the right, at the Harrison house pull-off. Step out of your vehicle and walk over to the historical signs.

GPS N 38° .130333 W 77° .361232

STOP 9: HARRISON HOUSE OVERLOOK

In the field across the road stood the house of Edgar Harrison, one of several farmers who lived on the Spotsylvania battlefield. Following the Union breakthrough at the Muleshoe Salient, Brig. Gen. John B. Gordon gathered his Confederate division at the house and prepared to lead it in a charge to retake the captured works. "All saw that a crisis was upon us," wrote one of Gordon's soldiers. "If we failed the consequence would be disastrous in the extreme. In this exigency, Gen. Lee rode forward in front of our line . . . . Not a word did he say, but simply took off his hat, and as he sat on his charger I never saw a man look so noble, or a spectacle so impressive."

Again, as he had in the Wilderness, Lee evinced a desire to personally lead his troops into combat. Again they turned him back. (FSNMP)

Gordon, seeing that Lee intended to lead the troops into battle himself, galloped over to his commander, seized the reins of his horse and shouted: "General these are Virginians! These men have never failed! They never will! Will you, boys?" From the ranks came cries of "No! no!" "Gen. Lee to the rear." "Go back!" "Go back!" "General Lee to the rear!" Stepping forward, a soldier took the reins of Lee's horse and personally led it to the rear, while Gordon led his men in a charge that succeeded in expelling the enemy from the eastern face of the Salient.

During the fighting that ensued, Lee made his headquarters near the Harrison house. Although he was able to contain the Union penetration, he realized

that he was not strong enough to retake the lost works. After midnight, he ordered Lt. Gen. Richard S. Ewell's corps to withdraw to a new line that Confederate engineers had constructed across the base of the Muleshoe, in the woods beyond the Harrison place. Lieutenant Colonel Theodore Lyman visited the new line after the war and was amazed by what he saw.

When Union troops broke through at the East Angle, Brig. Gen. John Gordon launched a counterattack from the vicinity of the Harrison house. Gordon recaptured the eastern face of the salient, but Federals held stubbornly to the apex. (FSNMP)

This was a curiosity of field fortifications! Warned by the dreadful loss & carnage of that day, exposed to an artillery enfilade from both flanks, and fearful of repetition of the terrible assault, the garrison worked with the energy & perseverance almost of despair! The high parapet was not only traversed as often as every 10 or 12 feet, but was enclosed on the rear, so that the line was divided into a series of square pens, with banks of earth heavily reveted with oak logs. From space to space was what looked like a wooden camp chimney, but in truth, an elevated post for sharpshooters, with a little loop hole in front. I never saw any like them.

For six days, Grant did not test Ewell's new line. Instead, he shifted his army east, toward the Fredericksburg Road. But on May 18, he doubled back, hoping to catch enemy napping. Instead, he found the Confederates ensconced safely behind their works, protected by a 100-yard-deep barrier of abatis that the Confederates had strewn across this field. Ignoring the obvious strength of Ewell's position, the II and VI corps pressed forward to the attack. Among those in the ranks was Pvt. James L. Bowen of the 37th Massachusetts. "It was a memorable scene. From right to left, for miles, the artillery crashed and roared; the woods and fields all about were filled with howling shot and bursting shell, to which the assailed made little reply. But it was not because they were dismayed or absent. Crouching behind their works they waited till the assailants should enter the abatis and become disorganized in the struggle through the slashings

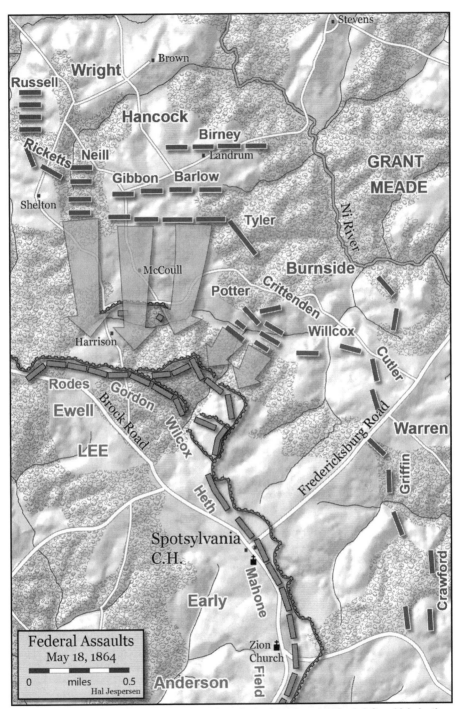

FEDERAL ASSAULTS, MAY 18—On May 18, Grant launched an attack against Lee's left—which, by then, was the area near the former Muleshoe—assuming that Confederates had weakened their line there in order to strengthen their right. However, the men of the Second Corps occupied that stretch of the line. They'd spent the days since creating the most extensive works yet seen in the East.

and impediments . . . . Then as the Confederate skirmishers were swept back before the strong lines of blue, the restrained tempest broke forth, and with shriek and scream and hissing, poured its death blast in the faces of the Union soldiers."

The 37th Massachusetts hugged the ground, hoping that other Union troops would turn the Confederates' flanks. But, as Bowen noted, "They waited in vain. The task undertaken was too trying, the slaughter would be too terribly certain, the prospect was too remote." Bowen's colonel gave the order to fall back. "We went in, lost some men and came out again—that is all there was to it!" commented one officer in the regiment. Bowen agreed. "No attempt ever more completely failed," he thought.

The Union army lost approximately 1,500 men that morning. Confederate losses, by contrast, were negligible. The following day, Meade penned a letter to his wife, in which he spoke about the assault. "We did not have the big battle which I expected yesterday," he wrote, "as, on advancing, we found the enemy so strongly entrenched that even Grant thought it useless to knock our heads against a brick wall, and directed a suspension of the attack. We shall now try to maneuver again, so as to draw the enemy out of his stronghold, and hope to have a fight with him before he can dig himself into an impregnable position."

Move up to the junction in front of you, turn left, and then turn left again onto the gravel road leading back to the McCoull house. Drive to the end.

GPS N 38° .131209 W 77° .360056

STOP 10: THE MCCOULL HOUSE

The McCoull House (FSNMP)

The stones at this site mark the outline of Neil McCoull's farmhouse, a building situated in the very center of the Muleshoe Salient. Major General Edward "Allegheny" Johnson used the house as his headquarters. Johnson commanded a division of Confederate troops that defended the Muleshoe Salient. He was at his headquarters on the night of May 11 when he noticed that the Confederate artillery that supported his position were moving to the rear. Later that night, Johnson received word that Union forces were massing in his front for an attack. He sent an urgent message back to his superior, General Ewell, pleading for the guns to be returned. Ewell granted Johnson's request, but by the time the artillery reached the front, Union soldiers were pouring over the works. Twenty of the cannon fell into Federal hands, most of them having not fired a shot.

Johnson and 3,000 of his soldiers became prisoners in the attack. The general was captured at the front, trying to hold back the Union army until the returning cannons could get into position. Captain William P. Carter commanded one of the Confederate batteries and witnessed the general's gallantry. "In the chill, misty, first early dawn of May 12, 1864, I saw a fine-looking, stout-built officer, clad in a long, gray military overcoat, rush on foot into the Horse Shoe salient . . . . As the officer would catch hold of and push away the bayonets of the storming enemy, I heard him repeatedly shout, 'Don't shoot into my men!' This was Major-General Edward Johnson, of Virginia . . . ."

Concerned at the removal of Confederate artillery from the Muleshoe on the night of May 11, Maj. Gen. Edward "Allegheny" Johnson implored that the guns be returned. They rolled back into position just in time to be captured. So was Johnson. Captured at the same time was Brig. Gen. George H. Steuart. The two officers were held as prisoners in the North but were later exchanged.
(FSNMP)

A party of Union soldiers escorted Johnson to General Hancock's headquarters in the rear. Captain Charles Brockway of Battery F, 1st Pennsylvania Artillery, was present when Johnson arrived. "Major General Johnson was brought in. He turned to his guard and courteously thanked them for their kindness. 'You are damned welcome,' was the blunt reply of the sergeant. Hancock greeted him cordially, saying: 'I am glad to see you, Ned.' 'Under other circumstances,' said the rebel, 'I would be pleased to meet you.'"

Turning to an aide, Hancock then said brusquely: "Telegraph to Warren and Burnside to attack at once; that I have routed Johnson and am going to roll up Early . . . ." "During these orders," wrote Brockway, "Johnson put his hand to his heart as though it pained him, and as he gazed upon his fellow prisoners and the earthworks, which, but an hour before were under his command, heavy tears coursed down his cheeks and his whole frame heaved with emotion. But he took a drink of liquor

Brig. Gen. John B. Gordon led the first Confederate counterattacks. "He's most the prettiest thing you ever did see on a field of fight," recalled one soldier. "It'ud put fight into a whipped chicken just to look a him!" (LOC)

with Hancock, who sent him on horseback to Grant's headquarters, accompanied by an aid[e]."

Return to the paved road and turn left. Drive 0.6 mile and stop at the east face of the Salient pull-off.

GPS N 38° .131445 W 77° .353581

STOP 11: EAST FACE OF THE SALIENT

The earthworks at this stop mark the east face of the Muleshoe Salient. Union infantry captured these works early on May 12 only to be driven from them a short time later by Gordon's Confederates. Gordon's men held this section of the line for the rest of the day as the fighting raged around the Bloody Angle.

A 600-yard trail leads from the parking area to the East Angle, located at the tip of the Muleshoe Salient. It was there that Union troops first penetrated the Confederate line. When you are ready, get back in your vehicle and drive 0.6 mile to a pull-off for Heth's Salient, on the right. Remain in your car.

GPS N 38° .125048 W 77° .531488

STOP 12: HETH'S SALIENT

A former professor at the Virginia Military Institute, James Lane had the misfortune of commanding the brigade that mortally wounded Stonewall Jackson. Despite an impressive combat record, especially at Spotsylvania, he never rose beyond brigade command. (SLOC)

In the woods to your right is Heth's Salient, an outward bulge on the east face of the larger Muleshoe Salient. Major General Henry Heth's division held this part of the Confederate line. On the afternoon of May 12, with the Bloody Angle fighting at an impasse, Grant looked for another avenue of attack. Thinking that Lee might have drawn troops away from Heth's Salient in order to reinforce the troops fighting at the Bloody Angle, Grant ordered Burnside to make an attack here.

Unaware of Grant's plans, Lee ordered Maj. Gen. Jubal A. Early, who was temporarily in command of A. P. Hill's Corps, to attack Burnside from the area of Heth's Salient. Confederate troops at the Bloody Angle were hard pressed, and Lee hoped that a diversionary attack against Burnside in this sector might relieve some of the pressure at the Angle.

At 2 p.m., Brig. Gen. James H. Lane's North Carolina brigade advanced from Heth's Salient, intent on capturing some Union batteries located off to your left. Colonel David A. Weisiger's Virginia brigade supported the attack. As Lane slid through the woods toward the Union batteries, he collided unexpectedly with elements of Brig. Gen. Orlando Willcox's division, which happened to be advancing to attack Heth's Salient. A confused scuffle ensued in this vicinity with soldiers grappling with one another at close range. Lane and Weisiger eventually drew off, returning to Heth's Salient with several hundred prisoners in tow, including nearly 100 men of the 17th Michigan. Their attack, while it failed to capture the Union batteries, threw Burnside's assault into disarray. For the rest of the day, the IX Corps would not play a significant role in the fighting.

Continue down the road two-thirds of a mile to the Fredericksburg Road pull-off, on the right.

GPS N 38° .124059 W 77° .343854

Maj. Gen. Henry Heth (pronounced Heeth) joined the Army of Northern Virginia in 1863 after serving in the West. He ably commanded a division in the Third Corps from Gettysburg to Appomattox. (LOC)

STOP 13: THE FREDERICKSBURG ROAD

In front of you is the Fredericksburg Road, modern Route 208, which runs between Fredericksburg, 10 miles to your left, and Spotsylvania Court House, one mile to your right. While the Army of the Potomac advanced on Spotsylvania Court House from the northwest, by way of the Brock Road, Maj. Gen. Ambrose E. Burnside's independent IX Corps approached the town from the northeast using this road. When Grant shifted his base of supply from Culpeper Court House to Belle Plains on the Potomac Creek on May 7, this road became his primary route of supply. Each day hundreds of wagons rolled south along the road, bringing tons of food, clothing, and ammunition to the Union army. Once they had disgorged their supplies, the wagons returned to Belle Plains by way of Fredericksburg, carrying wounded Union soldiers. "All empty wagons were positively jammed with men variously wounded," wrote sketch artist Edwin Forbes. "Single horses and mules bore the burden of two and three men upon their backs, and many lame soldiers limped along in pitiful fashion, offering to each other such assistance as was possible; so that between the battle-field and town a procession of misery, unequaled by any similar event of the war, passed slowly by."

Trapped in Fredericksburg by the rains with few supplies and little medical care, hundreds of Union soldiers perished. Burial scenes like this were common. (FSNMP)

Not all soldiers were fortunate enough to secure a berth in a wagon. Many had to make their way back to Fredericksburg on foot. Surgeon W. T. G. Morton passed hundreds of these men as he made his way to the front. "It is the most sickening sight of the war, this tide of the wounded flowing back," he wrote. "One has a shattered arm, and the sling in which he carries it is the same bloody rag the surgeon gave him the day of the battle; another has his head seamed and bandaged so you can scarcely see it, and he weaves like a drunken man as he drags along through the hot sun; another has his shoe cut off, and a great roll of rags wound around his foot, and he leans heavily on a rough cane broken from a pine tree; another breathes painfully and holds his hand to his side, where you see a ragged rent in his blouse; another sits by a puddle, dipping water on a wounded leg, which, for want of dressing since the battles, has become badly inflamed; another lies on a plat of grass by the roadside, with his browned face turned full to the sun, and he sleeps." Morton passed hundreds of such men in a matter of just a few miles. "They move along silently," he noted, "making no complaints, asking no questions and no favors of the passerby. Such heroic bravery and fortitude are only surpassed by their valor on the field of battle."

Continue forward to the Fredericksburg Road (Route 208). To go to the Harris farm, turn left and drive 1.4 miles. Turn left again when you reach Bloomsbury Lane (Route 1470). In 0.8 mile, keep straight ahead on Monument Court. Continue one-third mile farther and park on the right side of the road. To your right, on the ridge, is a monument. Walk up to the monument and, while standing there, face your car. This will be Stop 14.

GPS N 38° .140256 W 77° .341282.

If you wish to skip the Harris farm, turn right when you reach the Fredericksburg Road (Route 208) and drive one-quarter mile to the stoplight at Courthouse Road. Turn left at the light and drive another one-third mile to Spotsylvania Confederate Cemetery, on the left. Pull into the cemetery and park. This will be Stop 15.

GPS N 38° .120949 W 77° .345930

STOP 14: THE HARRIS FARM (OPTIONAL)

The May 12 fighting at the Bloody Angle ushered in five straight days of rain. "It looked as if Heaven were trying to wash up the blood as fast as the civilized barbarians were spilling it," thought Cpl. George M. Neese of the Confederate horse artillery. On May 17, the skies again cleared and military operations resumed. Hoping to catch Lee off guard, Grant on May 18 doubled back, attacking Ewell's Corps at the base of the Muleshoe Salient. The Confederates were ready for the assault, however, and beat it off handily. Undeterred, Grant continued to shift east, across the Fredericksburg Road.

During the May 19 fighting, Clement Harris's farm, "Bloomsbury," stood just behind Union lines and became a hospital. Engulfed by war in 1864, the farm was engulfed by development 150 years later. In December of 2014, the original farmhouse was finally torn down. (DP)

Unsure of his adversary's new position, Lee ordered Ewell to make a reconnaissance in force on May 19 to locate the right flank of Grant's shifting army. The two sides collided here late that afternoon on Clement Harris's farm, "Bloomsbury," used to stand 400 yards to your rear. Ewell's Confederates caught the Union army unprepared, briefly overrunning Union supply trains behind you, on the Fredericksburg Road, threatening Grant's line of communications with Washington.

Fortunately, Union reserves were near at hand. The previous day, Brig. Gen. Robert O. Tyler had reached the front with five regiments of heavy artillery fresh from the Washington, D.C., defenses. The "Heavies," as they were called, had been armed with rifles and would be fighting as infantry. Because they had not as yet been in combat, the regiments were large, numbering as many as 1,800 men.

Alerted to Ewell's approach, Tyler rushed the 1st Massachusetts Heavy Artillery into position on this knoll. Other heavy artillery regiments took position farther to your right, extending the Union line across the Alsop farm.

Although small in comparison to the May 12 fighting, the combat at the Harris and Alsop farms produced more than 2,500 casualties, including these men from Ewell's corps. (LOC)

Ewell's Confederates attacked from the low ground in front of you with their usual fury, initiating what one soldier termed a "desperate and determined" fight. To everyone's surprise, however,

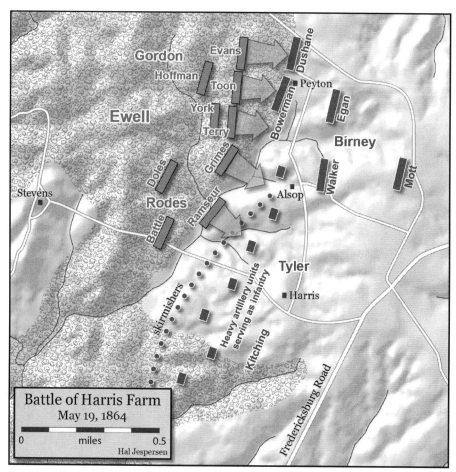

Battle of Harris Farm
May 19, 1864

0   miles   0.5
Hal Jespersen

BATTLE OF HARRIS FARM—While Confederates remained on the defensive for most of their time at Spotsylvania, Lee sent his Second Corps on a reconnaissance in force on May 19 to investigate the possibility of a strike on Grant's supply line along Fredericksburg Road. Near Harris farm, Lee's battle-hardened veterans found themselves up against green heavy artillery regiments new to the army. After some initial success, the Confederates quickly found themselves embroiled in combat that threatened to overwhelm them as even more fresh reinforcements to Grant's army streamed onto the battlefield for the first time and straight into the fight.

the Heavies held their own. The Confederates fell back only to come on again. Still Tyler's men refused to yield. The arrival of additional Union troops secured Grant's hold on the Fredericksburg Road, and, as darkness settled over the battlefield, Ewell's men withdrew to the Muleshoe. The Confederates lost 900 men in the action; the Federals, 1,500, more than a quarter of whom belonged to the 1st Massachusetts. It was the last major action at Spotsylvania Court House. The following day, Grant would begin moving toward the North Anna River.

Return to the Fredericksburg Road (Route 208). Turn right and proceed 1.7 miles to the stoplight at Courthouse Road. Turn left at the light and drive another one-third mile to Spotsylvania Confederate Cemetery, on the left. Pull into the cemetery and park.

GPS N 38° .120949 W 77° .345930

STOP 15: SPOTSYLVANIA CONFEDERATE CEMETERY

In two weeks of fighting at Spotsylvania Court House, the Union army lost more than 18,000 soldiers. Those who died are now buried at Fredericksburg National Cemetery. The Army of Northern Virginia, by comparison, lost an estimated 12,000 soldiers in killed, wounded, and missing. Six hundred of those soldiers are buried here.

Return to Route 208, turn left, and continue into Spotsylvania Court House. Park in front of the large administrative building that you'll see on the right side of the road before you reach the stoplight. A Civil War Trails sign marks the spot. Exhibits on the town and its role in the war are located in a small plaza located between the parking lot and the road.

GPS N 38° .120949 W 77° .345930

After the war, the Union dead were buried in national cemeteries funded by the United States Government. Southerners had to bury their own dead using private funds. Those who died at Spotsylvania were buried at a Confederate cemetery on the outskirts of the village. (DP)

STOP 16: SPOTSYLVANIA COURT HOUSE

In 1864, Spotsylvania Court House was a small town of no more than a few dozen inhabitants, boasting a courthouse, jail, hotel, and several churches. It was a busy place on court days or on Sundays when the faithful gathered for worship, but on most days it was a sleepy community, little different from dozens of other county seats across Virginia.

What made Spotsylvania important was its roads. For the armies fighting in the Wilderness, the roads that ran through the town represented the most direct route to Richmond. If Grant had been able to reach the town ahead of Lee, he would have had the inside track to the Confederate capital, forcing Lee to attack him in an effort to save Richmond from capture. Lee had won the race by the narrowest of margins, however, and he constructed formidable

At the time of the war, a well stood near the intersection in the town center. (FSNMP)

Spotsylvania was a sleepy village of a dozen or so buildings in 1860. Despite incurring shelling and vandalism, most of the wartime village still survives. (FSNMP)

earthworks around the town. For two weeks the armies battled here before moving on to fresh battlegrounds farther south. When they departed, they left behind a town battered by artillery fire and scarred by military occupation. Author John T. Trowbridge visited Spotsylvania little more than a year later.

> *We drove on to the Court-House: a goodly brick building, with heavy pillars in front, one of which had been broken off by a shell, leaving a corner of the portico hanging in the air. There were but six other buildings of any importance in the place,— one jail, one tavern, (no school-house,) one private dwelling, and three churches; all of brick and all more or less battered by artillery.*
>
> *Entering the Court-House amid heaps of rubbish which littered the yard about the doors, I had the good fortune to find the county clerk at his desk. He received me politely, and offered to show me about the building. It had been well riddled with shot and shell; but masons and carpenters were at work repairing damages; so that there was a prospect of the country, in a few months, having a court-house again.*
>
> *"What is most to be regretted," the clerk said, "is the destruction of documents which can't be restored. All the records and papers of the court were destroyed by the Union soldiers after they got possession." And he showed me a room heaped with the fragments. It looked like a room in a rag-man's warehouse.*

Given the damage to the town, it is surprising that any of the 1860s structures remain. That all of the major buildings mentioned by Trowbridge survive is nothing short of remarkable. Yet such is the case. Before leaving Spotsylvania, we encourage you take few minutes and explore the town.

Continue to the stoplight in the center of town. Turn left onto Route 613 (the Brock Road) and drive one-half mile to Zion Methodist Church, on your right.

GPS N 38° .113890 W 77° .351218

STOP 17: ZION METHODIST CHURCH

This brick sanctuary was just five years old at the time of the battle. Originally called Liberty Meeting House, the congregation had changed the name to Zion in 1861, perhaps to avoid the politically-charged overtones inspired by the word "liberty."

Situated just outside of town, Zion Methodist Church was used by Confederates as both a headquarters and an observation post during the battle. (DP)

Union soldiers briefly occupied the church in the summer of 1862 during a raid on the Virginia Central Railroad. Lieutenant Colonel Samuel Beardsley of the 24th New York took time to pen a letter to his father from the building's gallery. The church, he wrote, "is a perfect bedlam below as it is filled with soldiers, some scuffling, some whistling, some playing cards on the little plain table in front of the pulpit, while one independent gentleman in his shirt sleeves occupies the ministers chair in the pulpit and is engaged in the laudable occupation of combing his hair with a pocket comb while he occasionally stops to admire his handy work through the medium of a little pocket looking glass."

General Robert E. Lee occupied Zion two years later during the battle of Spotsylvania Court House. The general was sleeping on a board here on the morning of May 14 when a courier arrived with news that the Army of the Potomac had seized Myers Hill, a strategic hilltop just one mile away. Determined to retake the hill, Lee sent two brigades to regain it. They did, but the arrival of Union reinforcements compelled the Confederates to relinquish it a short time later.

Three days later, when Grant resumed his maneuvering, Lee ordered Brig. Gen. Ambrose R. Wright to make a reconnaissance towards

Myers Hill. A short distance down Massaponax Church Road, Wright encountered a strong line of Union pickets. After a brief skirmish, he brought his brigade of Georgians back to Zion Church. A. P. Hill, the ailing general, had witnessed Wright's lackluster performance and threatened to convene a court of inquiry to investigate the general's conduct. Lee met with Hill here at the church and tried to calm his excitable subordinate. "These men are not an army," he reminded Hill, "they are citizens defending their country. General Wright is not a soldier; he's a lawyer. I cannot do many things that I could do with a trained army. The soldiers know their duties better than the general officers do, and they have fought magnificently. Sometimes I would like to mask troops and then deploy them, but were I to give the proper order, the general officers would not understand it; so I have to make the best of what I have and lose much time in making dispositions." If Hill placed Wright under arrest, suggested Lee, the people of Georgia would not understand. "Besides," he asked, "whom would you put in his place? You'll have to do what I do: When a man makes a mistake, I call him to my tent, talk to him, and use the authority of my position to make him do the right thing the next time."

Turn right out of the parking lot and then immediately turn left onto Massaponax Church Road (Route 608). Drive 1.2 miles to Gunnery Hill Road (Route 1510). Pull into the dirt lot on the left, next to the intersection.

GPS N 38° .112381 W 77° .340645

STOP 18: MYERS HILL

The lane to your left, Gunnery Hill Road, leads back to Myers Hill, a rise contested by Union and Confederate forces on May 14. Following his May 12 assault on the Muleshoe, Grant began shifting his army south and east, hoping to turn Lee's right flank while at the same time maintaining his supply line with Fredericksburg and Belle Plains. After dark on May 13, Warren's V Corps slipped away from Laurel Hill, on the Union right flank, and slid behind the rest of the army until it reached the Fredericksburg Road. The VI Corps, under Brig. Gen. Horatio G. Wright, followed.

The plan was fraught with difficulty, as Warren's aide-de-camp, Maj. Washington Roebling, well knew. "We were expected to march all night, get into position on the left of Burnside's in an unknown country, in the midst of an Egyptian darkness, up to our knees in the mud, and assault the enemy's position, which we had never seen," he complained. Warren was informed of his route of march at the hour he was to begin moving. "I'll do the best I can," he promised, "but very difficult things are being attempted on these night movements over such roads."

For the men in the ranks, it was a dismal night. Wallowing up to their knees in mud along roads marked by small fires, Warren's weary men made slow progress. Captain George M. Barnard of the 18th Massachusetts remembered it as "a horrible night, all mud, rain, darkness, and misery." The troops slogged into position west of the Fredericksburg Road by midmorning, but they were in no condition to assault Lee's right flank, as Grant had hoped. Instead, Grant limited his objective for the day to capturing Myers Hill, a farm on the south side of the Ny River that overlooked the left wing of the Union army.

Brigadier General John Chambliss, Jr.'s Confederate cavalry brigade held the hill, but Grant was determined to change that. In the morning, he sent two V Corps regiments, supported by Emory Upton's VI Corps brigade to capture the hill. The Federals easily took the hill from Chambliss, but they had to relinquish it a short time later when two of Gen. Jubal Early's Confederate infantry brigades charged from the surrounding woods without warning. Meade had just left the hilltop a minute or two earlier and was and nearly captured. A Union soldier recalled: "About the middle of the afternoon, when a shower was at its height, Gen. Meade, accompanied by Gen. Wright . . . rode up to [the Myers house], entered it and sat down for a light conference . . . . The two generals had been conversing but a few minutes when the rattle of musketry from above started them. The next instant another volley nearer, accompanied with yells, was heard, and a number of bullets penetrated the house. Generals Meade and Wright had just time to rush out the rear doors and mount their horses

After John Sedgwick's death on May 9, Maj. Gen. Horatio Wright took command of the VI Corps. He remained in command of the corps until the end of the war. (LOC)

when the enemy came down upon the house and the troops around it like wolves . . . ."

The Confederates' success lasted only a few hours. Late in the afternoon, Meade marshaled a large force to retake the hill. When the Federals reached the crest, however, they found it abandoned. Realizing that he could not hold the position, Early had ordered his men back to their defenses near Zion Church.

Continue east on Massaponax Church Road (Route 608). In 3.7 miles you will come to a stoplight at Telegraph Road (Route 1). Just before you reach the stoplight, turn into Massaponax Church, on your left.

GPS N 38° .113639 W 77° .303534

STOP 19: MASSAPONAX CHURCH

Located along the busy Telegraph Road, Massaponax Church saw the passage of many troops. Graffiti of both Union and Confederate soldiers still scars its interior walls. (LOC)

Lee responded to General Grant's May 14 movement beyond the Fredericksburg Road by abandoning Laurel Hill and bringing Anderson's Corps to his right, extending the Confederate line beyond Zion Church. Thinking that Lee might have summoned Ewell's Corps to the right too, Grant doubled back on May 18 and attacked Lee's line below the Harrison house. Ewell's Confederates were still in place there, however and easily repulsed Grant's assault.

With Lee's army firmly entrenched across his front, Grant changed tactics. On May 20, he sent Hancock's II Corps to Milford Station, 16 miles to the southeast, to threaten Lee's lines of communication with Richmond. The Confederate commander had no choice but to abandon Spotsylvania Court House and head south.

Fearing that Lee might overpower Hancock's isolated corps, Grant set off in pursuit. The V Corps led the way, accompanied by Grant and Meade. The generals halted briefly here at Massaponax Church, where photographer Timothy O'Sullivan photographed them and their staffs seated on pews outside the building. They are the only pictures showing the two generals together.

From Massaponax Church, the V Corps turned south on the Telegraph Road (modern Route 1)— the most direct route to Richmond. When the

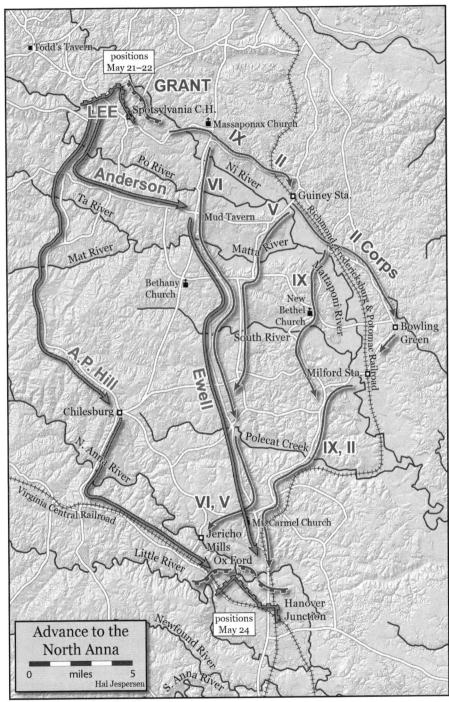

ADVANCE TO THE NORTH ANNA—Grant tried to lure Lee out of his works around Spotsylvania by dangling Hancock's II Corps as bait off to the southeast near Bowling Green. Lee declined to fall for it, instead marching south to take up a strong position along the south bank of the North Anna River. Lee maintained the tactical advantage but, with his back so close to Richmond, lost crucial room to maneuver.

Grant and Meade halted briefly at Massaponax Church en route to Guinea Station. In this iconic image, Grant is seen at left leaning over Meade's shoulder examining a map. (LOC)

Confederates blocked the way at the Ny River, however, Grant ordered Warren to turn east and head toward Guinea Station instead, thus keeping the Ny River between himself and the enemy. Wright's corps, then Burnside's, followed.

Proceed to the stoplight at Telegraph Road (Route 1), now called Jefferson Davis Highway. Turn right, and drive 0.6 mile. Turn left onto Guinea Station Road (Route 607) and drive another 0.6 mile to a Civil War Trails pull-off on the right. Face the road.

GPS N 38° .104970 W 77° .301367

STOP 20: STIRLING

The road in front of you leads to Guinea Station, formerly a stop on the Richmond, Fredericksburg, and Potomac Railroad. An ambulance carrying "Stonewall" Jackson used this road in May 1863 to carry the general to Guinea Station, where doctors intended to place him aboard a train bound for

Richmond. The general's condition deteriorated while at Guinea, however, and six days later he died there, his last words being, "Let us cross over the river and rest under the shade of the trees."

One year after Jackson's death, the Army of the Potomac trod this same road in its march to the North Anna River. On

the way they passed "Stirling," the impressive brick house in front of you. Built in 1858 by John Holladay, the structure features elements of both Federal and Greek Revival architecture. The outdoor kitchen and smokehouse are original to the house.

Country houses like Stirling attracted Union and Confederate soldiers alike and were often used by officers whose troops were camped in the area. (DP)

Brigadier General Ambrose ("Rans") Wright made his headquarters at the house during the winter of 1862–1863. His troops camped on the adjacent high ground, which they nicknamed "Hungry Hill" on account of the shortage of food they experienced while there. To supplement their meager rations, Wright's men stole livestock from the Holladay farm, including a flock of sheep and the owner's Newfoundland dog. When Holladay complained, Wright made a diligent search of the camp. He found the animals and arrested the thieves.

Later that day, Wright's men noticed an unusual amount of activity around the house and concluded that the general was hosting a large dinner party. After dark, a soldier cried out, "Who stole the dog?" to which another replied, "Company X, Third Georgia."

"Who eat the dog?" demanded the first man.

"Old Rans Wright and his staff," came the answer. Picking up on the joke, hundreds of soldiers spontaneously started to bark. Thereafter, the men of the 3rd Georgia insisted that Wright had it in for them, assigning them the hardest and most perilous tasks.

Stirling is one of five antebellum plantation houses still standing along this road. As you drive toward Guinea Station you will see the other four: La Vista, Westwood, Nyland, and Spring Grove. Each of these properties is privately owned. Please respect the owners' privacy and view the buildings from the road.

A citizen-soldier, Ambrose Wright began the war as colonel of the 3rd Georgia and ended it as a major general. (FSNMP)

Turn right onto Guinea Station Road (Route 607) and drive approximately three miles. At that point, Route 607 will turn sharply to the right. Follow it for two more miles to Stonewall Jackson Road (Route 606). Turn left on Route 606 and park in the gravel parking area just before you reach the railroad tracks.

GPS N 38° .083958 W 77° .262081

STOP 21: GUINEA STATION

Brig. Gen. Alfred Torbert's cavalry division led the Union advance to Milford Station.
(FSNMP)

Guinea Station was a stop on the Richmond, Fredericksburg, and Potomac Railroad. During the fighting in the Wilderness and at Spotsylvania Court House, it served as the Army of Northern Virginia's base of supply. The station stood near the point where the Po and Ny merged to form the Poni River. A rickety bridge crossed the swampy confluence one-half mile east of the station— behind you as you face the railroad. From there, it led due east a distance of four miles to Mud Tavern on the Telegraph Road.

A detachment of the 9th Virginia Cavalry was guarding Guinea Station at dawn, May 21, when Brig. Gen. Alfred T. A. Torbert's cavalry division, riding at the head of Hancock's column, appeared on Guinea Station Road. The Virginians fired off a few shots and then retreated down the railroad toward Bowling Green, leaving a detachment west of the river to guard the bridge. Rather than attempt to force a crossing there, Hancock assigned a force to guard the bridge and moved on.

That afternoon, Grant and Meade arrived at the station. The generals and their staffs had ridden ahead of the V Corps in hopes of catching up with Hancock, who was several miles ahead. When they reached Guinea Station, the generals found themselves far from either corps and vulnerable to a Confederate thrust across Guinea Bridge. When an officer suggested that they turn back and rejoin Warren, Grant proposed instead to hurry Warren forward. "Suggestions to the general to turn back fell as usual upon deaf ears," commented his aide, Lt. Col. Horace Porter.

Meade, meanwhile, ordered his headquarters guard, led by Brig. Gen. Marsena Patrick, to capture the bridge. As the Federal force approached, the

Confederates set fire to the span. Patrick's men splashed across the river and scattered its defenders and then doused the flames, saving the bridge for the army's use. Meade's aide, Maj. Washington Roebling, was impressed by the speed with which Patrick's men captured the structure. "The bridge was surrounded by swamps and dikes answering as breastworks," he wrote, and "the river was unfordable, so that even a moderate force could have held it for a long time; we were fortunate in forcing a passage so quickly."

Carefully cross the railroad tracks and immediately turn left onto the driveway leading back to the "Stonewall" Jackson Shrine. A Lee vs. Grant Trail sign is located near the restrooms.

GPS N 38° .085307 W 77° .262477

STOP 22: FAIRFIELD

Adjacent to the railroad and overlooking Guinea Station was "Fairfield," the 19th-century plantation house of Thomas Coleman Chandler. Next to the large brick dwelling stood the plantation office. Here, in April 1863, Gen. "Stonewall" Jackson first laid eyes on his infant daughter, Julia; and it was here, less than a month later, that he closed his eyes and spoke his final words.

Fairfield's main house (in the background) was close to falling down when a photographer took this picture in the early 20th century. However, the office building in which Stonewall Jackson died (in the foreground) was saved by Jackson admirers. (FSNMP)

Today, the house and surrounding grounds are administered by the National Park Service. Although the main house disappeared early in the 20th century, the frame office in which Jackson died remains. Exhibits and an audio program at the plaza next to the parking lot describe the property's importance. The building itself is open on a seasonal basis.

Return to Stonewall Jackson Road (Route 606) and turn left. In 0.6 mile, you will come to Rozell Road (Route 609). Park at the convenience store there and face Route 606, the road you were just traveling.

GPS N 38° .090605 W 77° .255564

Today the National Park Service administers the site where Fairfield once stood and where the house where Jackson died still stands. (DP)

STOP 23: MOTLEY HOUSE (PRIVATE PROPERTY)

Grant sat down for a smoke on the porch of the Motley house but left when its owner accused him of trying to burn down the building. (DP)

When General Grant arrived at Guinea Station, he set up headquarters in the yard of George Motley, an elderly man and a bitter rebel, who, according to Lyman, had "a certain sour dignity" about him. The Motley house stands in front of you, on the hill. While his staff pitched the headquarters tents behind the house, Grant took a seat on the Motley's porch and lit a cigar. Ashes from the cigar fell on the bench where Grant was seated, and when the wood started to smolder, the owner accused Grant of trying to burn down his house.

Not wishing to offend Motley further, Grant strolled down the hill and resumed his meditations at "Fairfield," the home of Motley's neighbor, Mrs. Chandler. The general and his hostess were soon chatting like two old friends. When Mrs. Chandler spoke of "Stonewall" Jackson's death there the previous year, Grant mentioned that he had attended school with Jackson at West Point and had later served with him in Mexico. "Then you must have known how good and great he was," said the lady. "Oh, yes," Grant replied, "He was a gallant soldier and a Christian gentleman, and I can understand fully the admiration your people have for him." After a few minutes Grant took leave of Mrs. Chandler, taking care to post a guard at the house so that no one would disturb her property.

Exit the parking lot and turn right onto Rozell Road (Route 609). Drive two and one-quarter miles to a field. Park where convenient.

GPS N 38° .073164 W 77° .244000

STOP 24: FIELDS

For two years, Meade's men had been fighting in northern Virginia, a region made desolate by war. But now, as they pushed south into Caroline County, they entered an area largely untouched by the conflict, an area teeming with crops and houses not yet ravaged by war. To one soldier, it seemed like "an earthly paradise," while another likened it to "a garden blooming in the midst of desert places." The refreshing scenery put the soldiers in a joyous mood. "The day was a warm and pleasant one," remembered one Federal, "and our march, through a country as fresh and bright as any we had seen since our march into Pennsylvania the year before, was more like a picnic excursion than a trial of speed with our enemy."

As the Union army moved south, its hungry soldiers ransacked the countryside, stealing at will from every farm that they passed. "Our army, operating in hostile territory, was like a swarm of locusts," wrote one soldier. "Hens, geese, chickens, ducks, and turkeys made a joyful sound, which found gleeful echoes in the neglected stomachs of tired soldiers."

As the army's provost marshal, General Patrick was responsible for preventing such depredations, but he could do little, for such actions were sanctioned by the general in chief himself. "We had a time, before Starting, in overhauling marauders & house plunderers," he confided to his diary on May 22, "some of whom I caught. Many complaints

As the army's provost marshal, Brig. Gen. Marsena Patrick was in charge of enforcing army discipline. He found it impossible to prevent soldiers from foraging, however, because Grant himself condoned it. (LOC)

After campaigning in war-torn northern Virginia for so long, central Virginia seemed like a paradise to the soldiers. Some celebrated their new surroundings by pillaging farms they passed. (FSNMP)

came to me & as I had a Culprit, I went to Meade, who told me that he really was unable to help me, that Grant had expressed himself strong against protecting these people at all, and I learned that his Staff were, themselves, engaged in sheep stealing, fowl stealing and the like . . . ."

Continue south on Rozell Road (Route 609) one-half mile farther to the Woodford Road (Route 626). Turn right and drive 1.1 miles to the Ni River. Park where convenient.

GPS N 38° .062066 W 77° .243449

STOP 25: DOWNER'S BRIDGE

On May 21, Warren crossed the Pony River at Guinea Bridge and headed west toward the Telegraph Road, followed by Wright. The next day, Burnside crossed the Mattapony River here at Downer's Bridge. (The Matta and the Pony rivers come together between Guinea Bridge and Downer's Bridge to form the Mattapony.) Meanwhile, Hancock remained hunkered down around Milford Station, four miles ahead of you.

This wartime sketch is labeled simply "Bridge across the Matapony river near Bowling Green Va." It may be Downer's Bridge. (FSNMP)

Six and one-half miles to the west (your right), the Army of Northern Virginia was strung out in a long column along the Telegraph Road, its soldiers marching briskly toward the North Anna River. The army's line of march took it directly across the front of Grant's converging columns, but in the absence of Sheridan's cavalry, which was on a raid toward Richmond, Union commanders did not appreciate the opportunity before them. "Here," wrote Warren's aide Roebling, "was a chance to capture the whole of Lee's wagon train; never was the want of Cavalry more painfully felt. Such opportunities are only presented once in a campaign and should not be lost." But the opportunity was lost. Worried that Lee might attack Warren's isolated corps, and lacking cavalry to provide him with proper intelligence, Grant allowed Lee to slip past him without molestation. Eleven months would pass before he would have another chance to deal the Confederate army such a lethal blow.

Proceed one mile and turn left onto South River Road (Route 638). Drive 0.8 mile farther to a gravel driveway on your left. Pause near the head of the driveway but do <u>not</u> go in. The house is privately owned.

GPS N 38° .050006 W 77° .250050

STOP 26: THE TYLER HOUSE (PRIVATE PROPERTY)

Grant and Meade bivouacked in the yard of the Tyler house on the night of May 22. (DP)

This massive brick plantation house was built by the Taliaferro family in the mid-18th century, but by the Civil War it was owned by the Tylers. Generals Grant and Meade pitched their tents in a clover field behind the house on May 22, having crossed the Pony River at Guinea Bridge earlier in the day. In the evening, as the IX Corps marched past the house en route to Bethel Church, its commander, General Burnside, turned aside to speak with them. Casting a sideward glance at his moving column, Burnside remarked pleasantly to Mrs. Tyler, "I don't suppose, madam, that you ever saw so many Yankee soldiers before."

"Oh, yes," she replied, "I have, many more." Obviously puzzled, Burnside asked where she had seen such a throng. Grant and his staff roared with laughter when the woman replied, "In Richmond," referring, of course, to the many Union soldiers being held prisoner there.

Continue south on South River Road (Route 638) for 0.8 mile to Bethel Church. Park in the church lot, on the right, just beyond the Route 605 intersection.

GPS N 38° .042070 W 77° .250898

STOP 27: BETHEL CHURCH

Bethel Church was just three years old when the Civil War disrupted the lives of its congregants. Although many of its male members went off to war, the assembly continued to worship here until January 1864 when circumstances forced it to close its doors. It resumed services in September 1865 and has continued in operation since that time.

The war invaded even the most secluded corners of Tidewater Virginia, even Bethel Church in rural Caroline County. (FSNMP)

A rarely published sketch of IX Corps commander Ambrose E. Burnside (FSNMP)

After crossing the Mattapony River at Downer's Bridge, Burnside's IX Corps bivouacked here on the night of May 22. An officer on Burnside's staff penned his sister a letter from the sanctuary. "After a long & continuous march of 24 hours we have encamped here & have just got washed & cleaned up," he wrote. "Our head Quarters are in a church, and many blankets are spread in the aisles . . . . As our troops came marching by the church . . . the Soldiers would say, Boys prayer meeting at 7 o'clock. Hello, here's a church fellows, let's go in & have a camp meeting. Another says, [']My house is the house of <u>God</u> but you have made it a den of thieves.' All seemed glad to see a church."

Burnside was then 40 years old. A Union soldier who happened to see him that week found the general "a much younger and more dashing looking man that I had supposed him." Burnside, he went on, "Wears side whiskers and moustache 'a la Militaire.' Wears a short roundabout coat and his pants in his boots and is altogether what the boys call a 'gay duck.'" Meade's aide, Theodore Lyman, was less charitable in his estimation of the general's appearance. After observing the general on May 23, Lyman wrote: "Burnside has a short military jacket, and, with his bell-crowned felt hat, the brim turned down presents an odd figure, the fat man!"

The general made himself at home in Bethel Church, where one of Meade's staff found him "sitting, like a comfortable abbot, in one of the pews, surrounded by his buckish Staff whose appearance is the reverse of clerical. Nothing," thought the writer, "can be queerer . . . than to see half a dozen men, of unmistakable New York *bon ton*, arrayed in soldier clothes, midst this desolated country . . . ."

Return to the intersection you just passed and turn right onto Paige Road (Route 605). Follow the road 2.9 miles to the railroad crossing. Pull over to the side of the road at the driveway you'll see on the right just before you reach the tracks.

GPS N 38° .033751 W 77° .223390

STOP 28: THE RICHMOND, FREDERICKSBURG, AND POTOMAC RAILROAD

The Richmond, Fredericksburg, and Potomac Railroad was Lee's primary line of supply during the Overland Campaign. Service on the line began in 1836, and by the following year it extended all the way from Richmond to Fredericksburg. Five years later it reached its northern terminus

at Aquia Landing, near the Potomac River. At an average speed of 13 miles per hour, it took five and one-half hours for a passenger to travel from one end of the line to the other.

Union troops encountered the railroad repeatedly on their march to the North Anna. One soldier remembered crossing the tracks no fewer than three times. That the Federals did not destroy the tracks clearly indicated Grant's determination to "take no backward steps."

Aquia Landing, just off the Potomac River, served as the Union army's base of supply in December 1862. Union soldiers wounded at Spotsylvania were shipped from there to Washington in May 1864. (LOC)

Continue straight ahead on Paige Road (Route 605) for one and one-quarter miles to the junction of the Fredericksburg Turnpike (Route 2). Turn right there and drive two-thirds of a mile into the town of Bowling Green. Park on the main street across from the courthouse.

GPS N 38° .030288 W 77° .205040

STOP 29: BOWLING GREEN

By the time Hancock's corps marched through here in 1864, Bowling Green had been the seat of government in Caroline County for more than 60 years. It was one of Virginia's most charming towns. "Bowling Green is one of the pleasant spots in this forlorn land," wrote a New York cavalryman in 1864. "Situated on . . . high ground, it commands a variety of rich scenery." A South Carolina artillerist, who wintered here with his battery, echoed the sentiment. "It is one of the beautifulist

GRANT TURNING LEE'S FLANK.

Grant's persistent efforts to turn Lee's flank prompted this *Harper's Weekly* cartoon. (LOC)

little vileges in Virginia," he wrote with admiration, if not with skill, adding that the town "affords some of the sweetest little girls I ever laid eyes on."

War had played sad havoc with the town, however. By the time Hancock's troops passed through in 1864, Bowling Green was but a shadow of its former self. "Great destitution was apparent everywhere," wrote one Union soldier, "and the inhabitants, composed almost entirely of women and children, were poorly and thinly clad, and hungry." The women, who had been so gracious to Southern soldiers a year before, had nothing but scorn for their foes. "Are you going 'on to Richmond'?" one sneered. "You'll all lay your bones in the ground before you get a sight of it."

Such comments antagonized the Federal soldiers and encouraged looting. Without shame, Pvt. Stephen W. Gordon, a soldier in the 15th New Jersey, admitted that his regiment not only pillaged Bowling Green but also almost burned it down. "[T]he whole army train passed through the town today," he noted in his diary under the date of May 23. "[T]his has been a very nice town before the war but is nearly deserted now. [T]he men are going through nearly every house. [T]hey have destroyed all of the old records in the court house, clerks and surrogates offices. I got a nice double barrel gun out of a store which I sold for fifteen dollars. Just at dark some of the men set fire to an old carriage shop and came near burning the whole town." Fortunately, the fire consumed few of the town's buildings.

Although it is much busier today than it was in 1860, Bowling Green retains much of its antebellum charm. A Lee vs. Grant Trail marker and a painting on the courthouse lawn identify some of the town's more notable structures.

Proceed to the next stoplight and turn right onto Milford Street. Drive one mile and turn left onto West Broaddus Avenue (Route 207). You will shortly come to a fork in the road. Keep to the right and merge onto Rogers Clark Boulevard (also Route 207). In less than one-half mile turn left onto Colonial Road (Route 722). Follow that road for one mile when it will bend to the left. Park in the dirt lot on the right side of the road.

GPS N 38° .012231 W 77° .222532

STOP 30: MILFORD STATION

You are now at Milford Station, another stop on the Richmond, Fredericksburg, and Potomac Railroad. You may be able to see the tracks on your right. In addition to its railroad depot, the village boasted a tavern, a distillery, and a few houses. The station was unprotected until May 20, when a party of 500 Confederate soldiers under Maj. George F. Norton, debarked at the station and set up camp nearby.

Norton's men were relaxing the next day when the sound of picket fire announced the approach of Hancock's corps. Fewer than 100 of Norton's men, led by Capt. Thomas B. Horton, took position on a hill one-half mile from the depot and prepared to fight it out. Confronting them was Brig. Gen. Alfred Torbert's entire cavalry division, which was leading the march of Hancock's column. Armed with repeating rifles, the Federals had an immense advantage not only in numbers but also firepower. "They kept up an incessant fire, having ammunition to spare, while we simply waited for targets among them," recalled one Southerner, adding, that "we made nearly every shot count."

Seeing that Horton was outnumbered, Norton ordered him to retreat, but the courier died before he could deliver the message. Too late, Horton realized that he was trapped. Gathering his men around he said, "Boys, you see our position. There is no escape. We will probably all be killed. But we will make them pay a big price for our lives. Be careful with your cartridges and make every shot count. If they charge us, it will soon all be over." He added: "We have taken [the hill] and will hold it as long as possible. It will give the brigade that much more time to save themselves." For several minutes, Horton's small band stubbornly held its position on the hilltop against long odds. But at last their ammunition ran out. Waving a towel in lieu of a white flag, the Confederates gave themselves up as prisoners of war.

Now unopposed, Torbert's troopers entered Milford Station and promptly set fire to the depot. Hancock's infantry arrived a short time later, forded the waist-deep water of the Mattapony, and established a good defensive position on the ridge beyond. The next move was up to Lee. Would he fall back to the North Anna River or try to attack Hancock's isolated command before Grant could come to his assistance? For Hancock, the next 24 hours would be stressful indeed.

Drive one-quarter mile to Nelson Hill Road (Route 722). Turn right and drive 2.2 miles. Turn left on Rogers Clark Boulevard (Route 207) and drive another 7.6 miles to the stoplight at Telegraph Road (Route 1). Stop along the shoulder of the road before you reach the light.

GPS N 37° .555264 W 77° .284778

STOP 31: THE TELEGRAPH ROAD

Established in 1847, the Telegraph Road (now Route 1) ran for 111 miles, between Washington, D.C., and Richmond, Virginia. As its name implies, a telegraph line ran the length of the road.

Anderson's and Ewell's corps of the Confederate army used this road in their march to the North Anna River. Lee's Third Corps moved to the North Anna by way of Chilesburg, several miles to the west. A. P. Hill again led the corps, having recovered from the illness he had contracted in the Wilderness.

Advancing from Milford Station, Winfield Hancock's II Corps struck the Telegraph Road about noon on May 23. But by then the rear of Lee's column had passed this point and was safely across the North Anna River. Turning to the left, Hancock pursued Lee south, directly down the Telegraph Road, while Warren veered off to the west, crossing the North Anna at Jericho Ford, four miles upstream.

This ends your tour of the Spotsylvania battlefield. To continue your tour of the Overland Campaign, cross Route 1 and take your first left onto Roundabout Road (Route 657). Follow the road back to Mount Carmel Church.

GPS N 37° .554684 W 77° .284966

The Bloody Angle at Spotsylvania (CM)

The North Anna River and Totopotomoy Creek

CHAPTER THREE

MAY 23-31, 1864

The North Anna River was a battlefield to Gen. Robert E. Lee's liking. He had wished to fight Burnside here in December 1862, but President Jefferson Davis had insisted that he defend the Rappahannock River line at Fredericksburg. Now, a year and a half later, Lee had no choice but to fight here. Lee's objection to fighting at Fredericksburg had been that the northern bank of the river, held by the Federals, dominated the southern bank, preventing him from making a successful counterattack. He could defeat the Federals on the Rappahannock, but he could not destroy them.

The North Anna River offered no such impediment. Here, the southern bank of the river dominated the northern bank in places, giving Lee the option to strike Lt. Gen. Ulysses S. Grant across the river if the opportunity offered. However, Lee would first have to defeat his adversary south of the river. To do so, he skillfully set a trap for the Union army—one that, if it had been properly sprung, might have ended Grant's "On to Richmond" drive and jeopardized President Abraham Lincoln's bid for reelection. That the trap remained unsprung is one of the great missed opportunities of the Civil War.

STOP 1: MOUNT CARMEL CHURCH

You are now at Mount Carmel Baptist Church, whose congregation dates back to 1773. Here, just three miles shy of the North Anna River, the different

For a year and a half, the railroad bridge across the North Anna River had been a vital link for supplying the Army of Northern Virginia. Ironically, the Confederates had to destroy the bridge in May 1864 in order to prevent the Army of the Potomac from using it as Grant's army pushed south. The brick pier and stone abutment of the original bridge still stand immediately adjacent to the modern railroad bridge, less than a quarter mile east of modern Route 1 on a road directly opposite the state historic marker at the south bank of the modern Rt. 1 bridge. (DP)

columns of the Union army converged. Warren's V Corps, marching south down the Telegraph Road, arrived first, at 9 a.m. Two hours later, Hancock's II Corps hove into sight from the direction of Milford Station. Wright's and Burnside's corps brought up the rear.

Mount Carmel Church (CM)

Grant and Meade made their headquarters at Mount Carmel Church on May 24. With them was Meade's chatty and observant aide, Lt. Col. Theodore Lyman. "We started quite early—a little before six—to go towards the North Anna," he wrote, "and halted at Mt. Carmel Church . . . . If you want a horrible hole for a halt, just pick out a Virginia church, at a Virginia cross-roads, after the bulk of an army has passed on a hot, dusty Virginia day!" Grant, Meade, and Meade's adjutant general, Seth Williams, occupied the building, where Lyman found them seated in the aisle writing dispatches on an ersatz table made from boards. To Lyman, "It looked precisely like a town-hall, where people are coming to vote, only the people had unaccountably put on very dusty uniforms."

While at the church, Grant received a dispatch from Maj. Gen. William Tecumseh Sherman, who was campaigning against Confederate forces in Georgia. According to Lyman, Sherman's note said "that the army of the west had fought enough to be entitled now to 'manoeuvre'; and that if Grant could inspire the Potomac army to do a proper degree of fighting, the final success could not be doubted." As Meade listened to the dispatch, "his grey eyes grew like a rattlesnake's," wrote Lyman. "Sir! I consider that dispatch an insult to the army I command, and to me personally," he snapped. "The army of the Potomac does not require General Grant's inspiration or any body's else [sic] inspiration to make it fight!!" According to Lyman, Meade "did not get over it all that day, and, at dinner, spoke of the western troops as 'an armed rabble.'"

Return to Route 1, turn right, and drive about two and a half miles to Long Creek. Just before you reach the creek, pull off to the right.

GPS N 37° .534294 W 77° .280297

STOP 2: LONG CREEK

In front of you lies Long Creek. Pressing south from Mount Carmel Church, Hancock's corps reached Long Creek at 2 p.m., May 23. Hancock approached the creek warily, believing it to be the North Anna River and expecting it to be staunchly defended. To his surprise, he discovered that the river was just knee deep and could be crossed by means of a ford rather than a bridge. More astonishing still, he found it undefended. Only after he gained the south shore did he realize that he was not at the North Anna but a tributary of it. The river itself still lay ahead.

Continue south just 0.3 mile and turn right on Oxford Road (Route 689). Drive one-third mile. On the way, you'll pass a modern brick house, on the left. The fort is approximately 150 yards beyond. This is Stop 3.

GPS N 37° .532667 W 77° .281545

It's little wonder Hancock's men mistook Long Creek (above) for the North Anna: on their march south, they'd crossed the Po and the Matta rivers, both of which looked no more formidable than the steep-banked but narrow Long Creek. (CM)

STOP 3: HENEGAN'S REDOUBT (PRIVATE PROPERTY)

On the left, at the edge of the woods, you may be able to see the front wall of an earthen fortification known as Henegan's Redoubt. Built in 1863 to protect Chesterfield Bridge against attack from Union raiders, the small, three-sided earthen fort had a 10-foot-tall wall bordered by an eight-foot-deep ditch. On this side of the redoubt was a 600-yard field extending to your right, toward Long Creek.

When Lee retreated to the south side of the North Anna River, he had left Col. John Henegan's South Carolina brigade (formerly Kershaw's) here to hold the redoubt. The 2nd South Carolina occupied the small fort, and the other regiments of Henegan's brigade entrenched in a line to either side of it. Henegan's men represented the only Confederate troops north of the river.

The Chesterfield Bridge (LOC)

Late on the afternoon of May 23, 3,000 men of Maj. Gen. David B. Birney's division of the II Corps arrived in front of the redoubt. At 6:30 p.m., they attacked. Henegan's men initially stood firm, pelting the oncoming Union lines with what one Union soldier thought of as "one of the most savage fires of shell and bullets I had ever experienced." According to another, "men in the blue-coated line fell headlong, or

Today, Henegan's Redoubt looks like little more than a snarly tangle of brush on the edge of a farmer's field, but the walls of the redoubt are easily visible. (CM)

backward, or sank into little heaps" crossing the field. But the Federals did not falter. Continuing forward, they reached the fort walls and began to scale them, jabbing bayonets into the face of the work to act like steps of a ladder while supporting the butt ends of the guns on their shoulders. Within seconds, the Federals surmounted the works. Trapped with their backs to the river, Henegan's men panicked. The South Carolinians broke for the bridge in "wild confusion," pursued closely by the Federals. About 200 Confederates were killed, wounded, or captured. At a cost of fewer than 300

Inside Henegan's Redoubt (LOC)

A sketch of Hancock's men as they crossed the North Anna (top); a photo of Union troops on the bridge (bottom). The antebellum stone piers of the original bridge still stand on the north and south banks of the North Anna River, about 300 yards upriver of the modern Route 1 bridge (below). (LOC; LOC; DP)

men, Grant now controlled the redoubt and the river crossings nearby.

Henegan's Redoubt is on private land. Please respect the owner's privacy and remain in your vehicle. When you are ready, turn around and return to Telegraph Road (Route 1). Turn right and drive one-quarter mile to the North Anna River. Pull over to the right at the state historical marker just beyond the span.

GPS N 37° .532172 W 77° .275858

STOP 4: THE NORTH ANNA RIVER

The North Anna River represented Lee's next line of defense. After capturing Henegan's Redoubt, the Army of the Potomac crossed the North Anna and for three days confronted Lee in his earthworks south of the river. Hancock crossed at Chesterfield Bridge near here; Warren and Wright negotiated

The tour specifies a stop on the south bank of the river, along the southbound lane, next to a historical marker that outlines a Revolutionary War story of Lafayette and Cornwallis; however, a historical marker along the northbound lane on the north bank of the river outlines the North Anna chapter of Lee vs. Grant. (CM)

A portion of the Union army crossed at Jericho Mills. (LOC)

the river at Jericho Mills, four miles upstream (to your right); and Burnside held the ground in between. An officer in Burnside's corps wrote that "Since leaving the Spotsylvania battle field, we have come on to this place without opposition, but find the Enemy posted here in force. I do not think it will be as fierce a contest here as on the Ny river, but they contest this ford with a good deal of obstinacy . . . . I hope we shall not be detained here long but keep on till we lay regular Siege to the Rebel Capital."

Less than one-half mile ahead, near the top of the hill on the right side of the road, is "Ellington," the wartime home of Parson Thomas H. Fox. On May 23, Lee was sitting on the front porch of the house drinking a glass of buttermilk when a Union artillery shell lodged in the door frame next to him. Lee calmly finished his drink, thanked his host, and departed. Soon after, Richard Anderson established his headquarters at the house. With him was Brig. Gen. E. Porter Alexander, who had charge of Anderson's artillery. As Alexander sat on the ground with his back against the sill of a basement window, a Union shell crashed into the chimney. It collapsed, killing two couriers. Alexander narrowly escaped the shower of bricks by pressing his back against the closed window behind him. The Fox house is now owned by the American Battlefield Trust but is not open to the public. Please do not enter the property.

The Fox house, "Ellington" (above). Lee sat on the porch as the battle opened. A collapsing chimney on the south side later killed a pair of couriers and nearly killed artillerist E. Porter Alexander. After crossing the river, Union soldiers ransacked the house. "A family library, containing some very rare and valuable works, was distributed through the corps," wrote one soldier, "and the walls of the house were ornamented with caricatures of Davis and the rebellion, and embellished with choice and pity advice to our 'erring sisters.'" (DP; CM)

To reach the next stop on the tour, continue south on Route 1 for a distance of two miles to Doswell, formerly known as Hanover Junction. Turn left there onto Doswell Road (Route 688) and drive 0.3 mile. Park after crossing the first set of railroad tracks.

GPS N 37° .513622 W 77° .273101

Confederates destroyed the railroad bridge over the North Anna in an attempt to prevent Grant from using it to move supplies in his southward march. Previously, it had been a vital link in the southern supply line. (LOC)

STOP 5: HANOVER JUNCTION

As Grant thrust southward from Spotsylvania, Lee maneuvered his forces to protect this vital railroad intersection. From here, the Richmond, Fredericksburg, and Potomac Railroad ran north and south, connecting Richmond with northern Virginia. The Virginia Central Railroad ran diagonally from Richmond northwest to Gordonsville where it intersected with the Orange and Alexandria Railroad. Daily trains rolled through this intersection with untold tons of rations, munitions, and clothing for Lee's army. Many of the returning trains were filled with sick and wounded soldiers destined for hospitals in Richmond or Charlottesville. Some of the men suffering from critical wounds or infectious diseases were left here at the junction to recuperate. In a letter penned on February 12, 1863, Confederate surgeon T. H. Wingfield noted that 200 patients were located at the junction, many suffering from smallpox.

The rail yard at Hanover Junction remains busy today. (CM)

Ahead of you, beyond the next set of railroad tracks, stood the town of Hanover Junction. It was as small in 1864 as it is now. All that was here then was an old hotel, several warehouses that doubled as makeshift hospitals, and a few railroad maintenance buildings. Railroad traffic was heavy at times, and wrecks and derailments were not uncommon. Sometime after the war the hotel

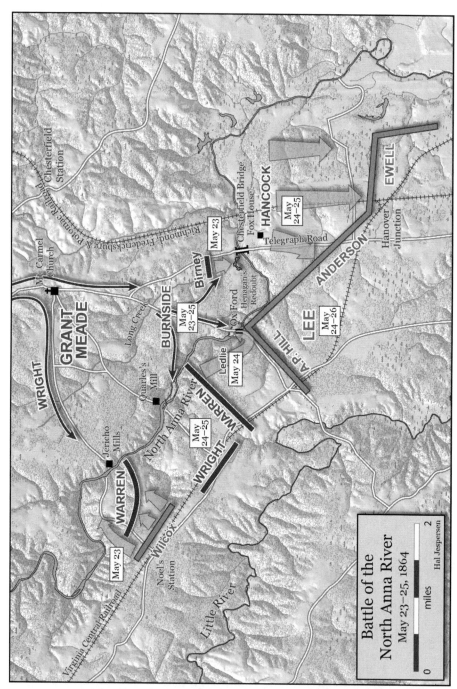

Battle of the North Anna River—The Union army's appearance at the North Anna River on May 23 took Lee by surprise. Before he could do anything about it, Barlow's division overran Henegan's Redoubt, north of the river, and Warren's corps gained a foothold south of the river at Jericho Mills. Lee countered by forming his line in the shape of an inverted "V" with its apex at Ox Ford. Grant probed Lee's new line, but only Ledlie's brigade attacked it.

and warehouses disappeared to make way for the quaint Victorian village that you see today. The name Hanover Junction was changed to Doswell, although many referred to it as Squashapenny for the pastime enjoyed by many Hanover youths.

It was approaching midmorning on May 22 when Lee arrived here and established his headquarters in a tent just southwest of the railroad intersection. The first order of business was directing his army to cross over the North Anna River and bivouac without fortifying. The Confederate army must remain mobile, Lee concluded, until Grant's precise route of march could be ascertained. Late on May 23, Grant's intentions became apparent. Heavy fighting on the Confederate left, near Jericho Mills, was evidence that the Union army was attempting to cross the North Anna. Lee resolved to hold the line and engineered one of the strongest defensive positions occupied by his army during the entire war. Formed in the shape of an inverted "V," with the point of the "V" resting on the high bank overlooking the North Anna, the flanks angled back, and each wing was in a position to be mutually supportive. Strong earthen fortifications made the position nearly impregnable. Hanover Junction was behind the line on the extreme right, or east side, of the "V."

Despite the strength of the Confederate position, the Federals attacked on May 24 and 25. The heaviest fighting in this sector occurred just north of here, on May 24, when the Union II Corps launched an attack along a wide front with the center roughly following the tracks of the R. F. & P. Railroad. Ewell's rough handling of this assault added to the mounting evidence that there was little hope for a Union victory here. A Union artillerist penned: "How we longed to

The Second Corps found itself emperiled but quickly dug in to protect itself. (LOC)

The Telegraph Road trace runs just inside a distant wood line visible from the state historic marker at the modern bridge across Route 1. During the war, the road ran on the west side of the Fox house, "Ellington." There is still a road there today. (DP)

The Federal pontoon bridge at Jericho Mills (LOC)

get away from the North Anna, where we had not the slightest chance of success."

Retrace your steps to Telegraph Road (Route 1), turn right, and drive one-third mile to Verdon Road (Route 684). If you wish to visit the area of the Jericho Mills combat (optional Tour Stop 6), continue on Verdon Road for 5.5 miles to Noel Road (Route 746). You are now near the site of Noel's Station. Turn right onto Noel Road and drive 0.6 mile when the paved road will end at a private gravel drive. Stop your car at that point and look down the gravel drive.

GPS N 37° .542846 W 77° .320694.

If you wish to skip the Jericho Mills stop, drive just 2.5 miles on Verdon Road (Route 684) to the entrance of North Anna River Battlefield Park. Drive back to the park.

GPS N 37° .525416 W 77° .295648

STOP 6: JERICHO MILLS (OPTIONAL)

Jericho Mills (LOC)

While Hancock was crossing the North Anna at Chesterfield Bridge, Warren's V Corps crossed without opposition at Jericho Mills, one-half mile to your left-front. Lulled into a false sense of security by Lee's lack of resistance at the river, Warren's men made camp and began to cook their dinners. The right end of the Union line was less than one-quarter mile to your left. Believing that he faced only Union cavalry, Maj. Gen. Cadmus M. Wilcox determined to attack. At 6:00 p.m., his division moved from right to left through this area. Lieutenant Colonel William J. ("Willie") Pegram's battery pounded the Union line, eliciting a savage response from 20 Union guns. Wrote one Union soldier: "The missiles screamed, shrieked, fluttered, whistled, and spitefully plunged with terrific force all around, over, before, behind, and everywhere else among the crouching soldiers; no place appeared to be secure from their devilish course . . . ." Wilcox's unexpected attack drove in Warren's pickets and succeeded in turning the Union right flank, in the area to your left rear. "They flanked us on the right," recalled one Union officer, "and such running your never saw."

Union engineers build a road from the crossing point at Jericho Mills. (LOC)

Panic set in, and Warren's entire line began to unravel as troops fled for the safety of the river. It looked as if it was to be another Ball's Bluff. Fortunately, three batteries of Union artillery still stood between the Confederates and the Union pontoon bridges. As they unleashed canister into the onrushing gray ranks, a small body of Union infantry mounted a counterattack. Stunned by the fury of the artillery bombardment and surprised by the unexpected Union counterthrust, the Confederates now panicked and gave way. "The singular spectacle was exhibited of two opposing lines giving way at the same time," Wilcox wrote.

Unaware of the size of the Confederate force in front of him, Warren chose not to pursue. Instead, his troops entrenched. Although Heth's division was near at hand, A. P. Hill too chose not to renew the fight. Lee later chided him for that decision, snapping, "Why didn't you throw your whole force on them and drive them back as Jackson would have done?" Realizing that the opportunity for destroying Warren's isolated corps had passed, Lee drew in his left flank and threw it across the railroad, creating the left arm of his inverted "V"-shaped line. He had set the trap. But would Grant walk into it?

Make a U-turn and return to Verdon Road (Route 684). Turn left and drive three miles. Turn left and follow the road back to North Anna Battlefield Park.

GPS N 37° .525416 W 77° .295648

STOP 7: NORTH ANNA BATTLEFIELD PARK

Once Grant secured a lodgment south of the river at Jericho Mills, Lee pulled back the flanks of his army, forming his line into the shape of an inverted "V" with its apex at Ox Ford and awaited attack.

Believing that Lee was in retreat, Grant and Meade ordered the entire army to cross the river in pursuit. On May 24, Wright's VI Corps followed Warren across Jericho Ford, while Hancock's II Corps crossed downriver at Chesterfield Bridge. Burnside alone found the going difficult. When his IX Corps attempted to cross the North Anna at Ox Ford, it found Confederates blocking its path. Believing the Southerners to be merely a rear guard, Burnside ordered a division across the river on either side of Ox Ford in the hope of cutting off the retreat of the enemy force. But when a Union brigade led by Brig. Gen. James H. Ledlie probed the Confederate position near the ford, it found the line manned and heavily entrenched. Despite orders to exercise caution, a drunken Ledlie ordered his troops forward into the face of the Confederate guns, losing 450 men.

The North Anna Battlefield Park, administered by Hanover County, opened in 1996 after a local gravel company preserved 80 acres of the core battlefield and installed hiking trails. (CM)

Ledlie's improvident charge opened Grant's eyes to the danger. With his back against the river and the wings of his army separated by a distance of six miles, it was now Grant rather than Lee who found himself in peril. As the sun dropped toward the western horizon, Grant halted his pursuit and ordered the Union army to entrench. Once again, Lee had thwarted his designs.

The field over which Ledlie attacked, in addition to much of Lee's V-shaped line, is protected by North Anna Battlefield Park. Managed by Hanover County, the park has a superb walking trail with many interpretive exhibits. If you have the time, we encourage you to take it.

After visiting the park, retrace your steps to Hanover Junction by turning left on Verdon Road (Route 684), driving 2.5 miles, and turning right onto Telegraph Road (Route 1). Drive one-third mile, turn left on Doswell Road (Route

688), and drive another one-third mile. This will bring you back to Hanover Junction. Continue driving east on Route 688 for just over one-tenth of a mile. There, Route 688 makes a sharp turn to the right. Take that turn and follow the road south a distance of 1.2 miles to the intersection of Route 30, the site of Garnett's Crossing. Turn left (east) onto Route 30 and find a place to park. The historic roadbed ran just to the west of the current road.

GPS N 37° .505509 W 77° .63922

STOP 8: THE CONFEDERATE RIGHT FLANK

Lee determined that Hanover Junction must be held at all costs. The right flank of his inverted "V" line wrapped around Hanover Junction and extended southward along the road you have been traveling. Early's division of Ewell's Corps prepared a line of fortifications that ran slightly east and generally parallel to the road. Adding to the defensibility of this sector of the Confederate line was an uninviting swamp, where a group of Confederate pickets found themselves uncomfortably posted "half a leg deep in mud and water."

With the close proximity of the Richmond, Fredericksburg and Potomac Railroad, the opportunity arose to reinforce certain Virginia units with rear echelon troops from Richmond. One of the benefitting organizations was Parker's Battery. When the green troops detrained, a veteran of the battery must have coaxed some laughter from his fellow artillerymen when he asked a replacement just how long they might be with Lee's army. "I don't know," the naive recruit responded, "but we can't stay over Sunday anyhow, for we didn't bring any clean clothes with us."

Continue east on Route 30. Drive 1.1 miles to the crossing of the North Anna at Maurice's Bridge. Pull off the road beyond the bridge at the state historic marker.

GPS N 37° .505989 W 77° .253923

STOP 9: MAURICE'S BRIDGE

At the time of the war, this was known as Maurice's bridge, after a local landowner. Although

not directly connected to the Overland Campaign story, Confederate forces burned the bridge here on July 2, 1863, to impede the progress of a Union cavalry and infantry raid. The Federal raiders left Fort Monroe with orders to destroy railroad bridges and disrupt Lee's lines of communication with Richmond as the Gettysburg campaign unfolded. They accomplished their basic mission and, in addition, collected information about the King William and Hanover County road network, information that benefited the Union cavalry charged with screening Grant's march to the Pamunkey in 1864.

Confederate forces burned Maurice's Bridge in July of 1863 in an effort to stymie a Union cavalry raid. (LOC)

Proceed on Route 30 a distance of 3.5 miles to the crossing of Route 2/301. Cross over the road and park beyond, where you see the Civil War Trails sign.

GPS N 37° .500453 W 77° .221005

INTERLUDE: UNION DISENGAGEMENT FROM THE NORTH ANNA

By May 25, Grant realized that Lee's army was firmly entrenched and unassailable. He pondered his options and came to the conclusion that a march around Lee's right, to the southeast, was his best option. If he could maneuver the Confederate army into the open, he could perhaps engage it in a decisive and final battle. Lee's failure to attack the Army of the Potomac, when it was divided by the North Anna River, convinced Grant that the Confederate army was on its last legs. He confidently wrote Chief of Staff Henry W. Halleck: "Lee's army is really whipped. The prisoners we now take show it, and the actions of his army show it unmistakably. A battle with them outside of entrenchments cannot be had. Our men feel that they have gained the morale over the enemy and

Union troops entrenched on the south bank of the North Anna River once Grant recognized the trap his army had stumbled into. He realized he needed to quickly extricate his men and once more swing around Lee. (LOC)

attack with confidence. I may be mistaken, but I feel that our success over Lee's army is already assured."

Grant's plan required that the Union army disengage from Lee without inviting attack. Despite the danger in such an undertaking, the Union army was expert at this type of extrication, having performed it twice before during the month, first at the Wilderness and then at Spotsylvania. Moving beyond the North Anna was unique in that the march would be dramatically longer and, more importantly, the roads were not scouted and relatively unmapped. Could the tired army survive another forced march? Would Lee react with his customary alacrity? The answers to these questions would determine the success of the operation. Within the army there was no clear consensus. The head of the V Corps artillery wrote: "Can it be that this is the sum of our lieutenant general's abilities? Has he no other resource in tactics? Or is it sheer obstinacy? Three times he has tried this move, around Lee's right, and three times has been foiled."

A series of generally parallel roads moving southeast in theory could carry the army to the Pamunkey River, where it would cross into Hanover County, a region familiar to the veterans of McClellan's 1862 campaign. The army's base of supply would shift to White House Landing on the

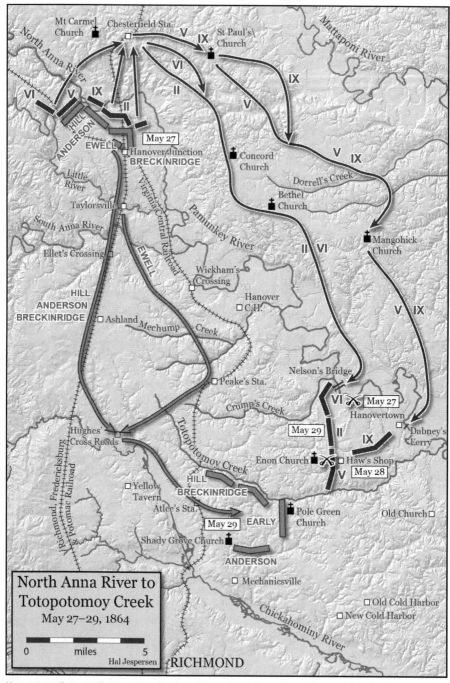

North Anna River to Totopotomoy Creek
May 27–29, 1864

0 — miles — 5
Hal Jespersen

NORTH ANNA RIVER TO TOTOPOTOMOY CREEK—After several days of sparring, probing, and maneuvering, the Army of the Potomac pulled away from Lee's lines along the North Anna River and again moved beyond the Confederate right flank. Grant's objective this time was the Pamunkey River, which he crossed in two locations. Cavalry screened his movements and clashed with their Confederate counterparts on several occasions. Lee, meanwhile, countered Grant's move by swinging south and taking up another strong defensive position along the steep southern bank of Totopotomoy Creek.

Pamunkey. If the Union army acted quickly and with stealth, Grant's ultimate objective of forcing the Confederate army to fight on a battlefield not of Lee's choosing was possible.

The pullout began after dark on May 26. The success of the Union operation rested on the shoulders of the army's temperamental and pugnacious cavalry commander, Maj. Gen. Philip H. Sheridan. While the infantry disengaged, a contingent of Sheridan's troopers performed deceptive demonstrations at the various crossings on the North Anna. The balance of the Union cavalry headed southeast for the Pamunkey River where it was to further confuse Lee by picketing the various crossings there. The first Union infantry to leave the North Anna was Russell's VI Corps division. Escorted by cavalry and accompanied by engineers and a pontoon train, Russell's men marched directly for Dabney's Ferry at Hanovertown and secured a bridgehead. The rest of the army was a day behind. Plans called for the main army to begin arriving at the Pamunkey late on May 27 or on the morning of May 28.

The North Anna evacuation went remarkably well despite heavy storms that turned the roads into what an eyewitness described as a "knee-deep, a little thicker than soup," muddy morass. By the morning of May 27, most of the Union army had pulled back toward Mount Carmel Church, a landmark they had passed four days earlier on the way to the North Anna. From there, they marched east several miles to Chesterfield Station on the Richmond, Fredericksburg & Potomac Railroad where they received rations and ammunition.

Grant's original plan directed that the Union vanguard leave the station early on May 27. The four corps were divided into two columns, each column following a different route to the Pamunkey River. The V and VI corps were to cross the river at New Castle, and the II and IX corps would cross at Dabney's Ferry. Once the march got underway, new orders were issued redirecting the II Corps to follow the VI Corps on the roads closest to the Pamunkey and then cross at Nelson's Ford two miles upriver from Hanovertown. Grant and Meade decided to accompany this wing of the army. The IX Corps was to follow the V Corps on the roads north and east of the other two corps and then turn southeast

"I FEEL THAT OUR SUCCESS OVER LEE'S ARMY IS ALREADY ASSURED."

— U. S. GRANT

toward Mangohick Church. The march began on a positive note, according to Grant's aide, Lt. Col. Horace Porter. "On the march the general-in-chief, as he rode by, was vociferously cheered, as usual, by the troops. Every movement directed by him inspired the men with new confidence in his ability and his watchfulness over their interests . . . ." Not just the officers, but the men in the ranks, too, "understood fully that he had saved them on the North Anna from the slaughter which would probably have occurred if they had been thrown against Lee's formidable intrenchments, and had had to fight a battle with their backs to a river; that he had skillfully withdrawn them without the loss of a man or a wagon, and that they were again making an advance movement."

The entire route to the Pamunkey River was more than 30 miles. Any pleasant thoughts that the men had at the commencement of the march were dispelled by the physical exertions of the long, hard drive. Abnormally hot weather, combined with muddy roads and horrific traffic jams, made the march one of the most infamous in the annals of the Army of the Potomac. "It was small wonder that men were prostrated by weakness, and overcome by the fierce heat that beat upon their devoted heads so pitilessly," a veteran from Maine remembered. "Some staggered blindly out of column, and sank down upon the roadside, to die there upon the dust-whitened grass, from the deadly sunstroke, no less fatal in its effect than the bullet." One Massachusetts soldier was "persuaded that if all the regiment were to be summoned—the living and the dead—and notified that all their marches except one must be performed over again, and that they might choose which one should be omitted, the almost unanimous cry would be, 'Deliver us from the accursed march along the Pamunkey!'" The trail you will take to the Pamunkey River incorporates segments of the routes followed by the Union army.

STOP 10: RICHMOND-FREDERICKSBURG STAGE ROAD (DAWN INTERSECTION)

You just crossed the Richmond-Fredericksburg Stage Road, modern Route 2/301. Over the years, traffic engineers straightened much of the historic road that had provided colonial travelers a relatively direct route between Richmond and Northern Virginia. Travel between Fredericksburg and Richmond in the 18th and early 19th centuries could take more than a day if the road was difficult.

The completion of the Richmond, Fredericksburg & Potomac Railroad in 1836 offered travelers a quicker and easier journey, and the stage company operating on this road soon went out of business. The road you are currently on, Route 30, was known historically as the Ridge Road. It ran through the heart of King William County. During the Civil War, a few residences and a country store near this intersection comprised a hamlet called Bowersville, which was later changed to Dawn.

Union cavalry led the way through this intersection as the Union army continued its inexorable march southward. (CM)

It was approaching darkness on May 26 when Phil Sheridan led two divisions of Union cavalry under Brig. Gen. Alfred T .A. Torbert and Brig. Gen. David M. Gregg through this intersection. Earlier in the day they had mounted up near Chesterfield Station and started for the Pamunkey River, where they were to secure crossings for the infantry, who would follow the next morning. When they arrived here, several companies under Gregg were ordered to follow the stage road (Route 301) south toward Hanover Court House, where Littlepage Bridge crossed the Pamunkey River. They were to guard the crossing to prevent Confederate cavalry from intercepting any of the Union columns. Sheridan and the rest of his troopers continued east along the Ridge Road in the direction of Mangohick Church.

Right on schedule, the Union infantry of Wright's VI Corps began arriving at this intersection late in the afternoon of May 27. Like the cavalry, they also turned east on the Ridge Road for what became the last leg of a punishing march that lasted well into the night. Wright's orders were to stop and camp just a few miles short of Nelson's Crossing on the Pamunkey.

As the shadows lengthened, Hancock's II Corps infantry and artillery poured through this intersection behind the VI Corps. Hancock's initial orders were to bivouac two miles north of this intersection at Concord Church, then start his march for the Pamunkey early the next morning, May 28. Instead, the hearty II Corps men took a short rest at the church and then pushed ahead in an effort to keep up with the VI Corps. Despite the urgings of the officers to keep the columns moving, a great deal of foraging occurred. "The county we passed through was new to us and well supplied with sheep, pigs, poultry, etc.," according to a member of the 9th Massachusetts. "Our marching columns 'traveled on their bellies,' for there was much foraging and cooking indulged in to the great chagrin of the natives and owners of the aforesaid live stock." Disgusted and angry, Ella Washington gazed from her residence as the Union columns passed bearing food for their evening feast. "We see them passing all day with sheep, hogs, veal and fowls; with quarters of mutton and beef hung to poles which they carry between them," she wrote. "They have even taken the servants fowls and pigs. Certainly there was never such an army of demons collected before, outside of the infernal regions."

Continue east on Route 30 a distance of 1.4 miles and pull into the Bethel Church parking lot, on your right.

GPS N 37° .493775 W 77° .204241

STOP 11: BETHEL CHURCH

Bethel Church (CM)

This small brick Methodist sanctuary was only six years old when Virginia seceded from the Union. Three years later, on the evening of May 27, 1864, General Hancock paused here long enough to refer to the church as his headquarters in official correspondence. The road in front of the church was filled with tired soldiers slogging ahead in almost total darkness. In patented Hancock form, he assessed the situation and, despite the option to halt his corps at nightfall, he directed his men to press on another five miles and camp close by the VI Corps at McDowell's Mill. Hancock's desire to push his fatigued troops ahead through the night meant that the two corps would be in supporting distance of each other, and the next days' march to the Pamunkey would be considerably easier. A courier rode ahead to army headquarters at Mangohick Church to notify Grant and Meade of the decision. Hancock's dispatch also informed Grant that several slaves reported Lee's army to be leaving Hanover Junction and heading south on the Richmond road.

Turn right out of the church parking lot and continue east on Route 30 for 2.6 miles to the Calno Road (Route 601), which led to Nelson's Ford. Pull over to the right just after you pass this road.

GPS N 37° .484861 W 77° .180706

STOP 12: CALNO

The original orders were for the II and VI corps to march through this intersection and then on to Mangohick Church, about a mile and a half in front of you. Mangohick was also the destination of the V and IX corps, which were just then marching on parallel roads to the north, your left. Mangohick could potentially become a bottleneck, creating untold congestion and confusion. To remedy this, Meade directed the II and VI corps to turn south here and camp at McDowell's Mill, about two and a half miles to your right. From there they would have an easy two- to three-hour march to Nelson's Ford the next morning.

In the late afternoon of May 27 and continuing late into the night, first the VI then the II corps made the turn here on their way to their evening bivouac. The day's march had been long and grueling. A veteran of the 7th New Hampshire recalled: "On and on, through all the long, hot afternoon, with slow but constant progress they marked the hours. At sunset there was a brief halt for coffee, but it was long past midnight when the men threw themselves on the ground to snatch a few hours' rest." To a Pennsylvania soldier, the long, tedious march was offset by the realization that they "did not hear the report of a canon to-day for the first time since the 5th of May."

Pull back onto Route 30 and drive 1.6 miles to Mangohick Church Road, on the right. Pull down the road and park in the church lot.

GPS N 37° .483540 W 77° .162507

STOP 13: MANGOHICK CHURCH

Mangohick Church (CM)

By American standards, this colonial sanctuary that dates to about 1730 was already ancient at the time the armies arrived here in 1864. Its Native American name is shared by a nearby stream. The neighboring community that went by the same name consisted of a store, blacksmith shop, a gig maker, shoemaker, and tailor's shop. Union Provost Marshal Brig. Gen. Marsena R. Patrick observed that "The Old Church is a curiosity, built in old times, when Virginia was a loyal Colony of the British Crown & brought bricks from England to build here loyal churches. This church seems to have passed thro' various hands," he noted, "& is now out of order, the rebels having used it for a Forage Depot since the War."

Around 1:00 p.m. on May 27, Grant and Meade rode into the churchyard. Meade selected the nearby Thompson house as his headquarters, where the family's patriarch took the opportunity to launch into the army commander about foragers stealing his supplies. Grant, suffering from a severe migraine, retired to a nearby tent, where his doctors applied a chloroform treatment. As the day was rather warm, the headquarters staff found sanctuary in and around the building. A Wisconsin soldier who happened by reported that "a number of the pews had been carried out and placed under the trees, and in them were a number of officers resting, some of them stretched out on the hard seats, with their hats over their faces, sound asleep."

Couriers arrived regularly with encouraging reports. The V and IX corps commanders announced their arrival about a mile north of

Mangohick, where they had gone into camp. Their infantry would be rested in time for the final push to the Pamunkey, scheduled for the next morning. To the south, Sheridan's cavalry took the Hanovertown crossing, and engineers had successfully spanned the Pamunkey with pontoons. Elements of the VI Corps were marching into Hanover County. Telegrams to the Secretary of War in Washington captured the exhilaration felt by the Union field commanders. They announced that the campaign was proceeding just as planned. Unsaid, however, was the question that doubtless perplexed Grant: Where was Lee?

Continue east on Route 30 for one mile to Hebron Church, on the left. Pull into the church parking lot.

GPS N 37° .480218 W 77° .153714

INTERLUDE: LEE'S COUNTERMOVEMENT TO BLOCK GRANT'S ADVANCE ON RICHMOND

Early on the morning of May 27, Lee discovered that Grant had abandoned his North Anna position. Reports also arrived from Confederate cavalry outposts along the Pamunkey River that Federal cavalry were crossing in sizable numbers at Hanovertown. Having initially fallen for Grant's deceptions, Lee reacted with his usual swiftness and issued orders for an immediate withdrawal. By 10:00 a.m., his army was in motion. It stretched interminably along three parallel routes heading south, deeper into Hanover County.

Based on the May 23 journal entry of Lee's staff officer, Col. Walter Taylor, Grant's assessment about the poor condition and morale of Lee's army as they moved south is questionable. "No doubt the entire north is this day rejoicing over our retreat to this point," he wrote, "yet the battlefield was left in our possession, and we marched here without any molestation whatever. This does not look like a retreat. Our army is in excellent condition; its morale as good as when we met Grant—two weeks since—for the first time. He will feel us again before he reaches his prize."

Nevertheless, a retreat under any condition challenged the most stalwart. "They marched in such deep silence," recorded Porter Alexander, "that a man with his eyes shut would only have known that any one was on the road by the occasional rattle of a canteen." The muddy conditions of the roads combined with the oppressive heat to make matters even worse. Roads deteriorated into bogs. Artillerists repeatedly pried their guns from the muddy depths that threatened to swallow them up. Except for the occasional women waving handkerchiefs at the passing columns of infantry, there was little celebration.

Lee's destination was a line along the watercourse known as Totopotomoy Creek. Due to the late start on May 27, it was not until early on May 28 that the Confederate army moved into position along the ridge that overlooked the creek's meandering, swampy valley. Lee's left rested on the Virginia Central Railroad, just north of Atlee Station. The remainder of the army stretched nearly five miles to the east with its right near Polegreen Church. The soldiers hastily dug breastworks along most of the line. Lee's defensive arrangement along the Totopotomoy allowed flexibility for a quick adjustment depending on Grant's chosen route of march. Lee knew he was slightly south of Grant and in a good position to protect the railroads and Richmond, but he desperately needed better, more precise information about the Union army's movements.

Early on May 28, Lee directed his cavalry commander, Maj. Gen. Wade Hampton, to lead 4,500 troopers on a reconnaissance to find Grant's army. Hampton's orders were to ride east toward Haw's Shop. At the same moment, Brig. Gen. David M. Gregg ordered his Union horsemen to mount up and strike for precisely the same destination. The need for information by both sides set the stage for one of the war's epic cavalry engagements.

STOP 14: HEBRON CHURCH

The morning of May 28 was sunny and cool. Infantry of the V and IX corps awoke early, downed the necessary sustenance, and began a march that took them past Mangohick Church. Near 7:00 a.m. Griffin's division, leading the V Corps, passed here "with bands playing and men in good spirits cheering," recalled the diarist Lyman. The lead elements of the V Corps turned south at this intersection, then east (left) at the forks in the road. The march to the crossing would take about three hours. The troops passed the little town of Enfield on their way to the Hanovertown pontoon bridges. Following behind the V Corps was the infantry of Gen. Ambrose Burnside's IX Corps. As you drive the quiet, narrow country road, try to imagine the scene in 1864: one column of soldiers marching in the road and a column on either side. "Few people can witness the spectacle unless they belong to it," one Connecticut soldier wrote. "A simple division seems to fill the country, and an army corps with its masses of men—batteries, supply trains, cavalry, etc.,—as it goes swarming over all the roads and byroads, and through the fields and woods, really does cover the entire area within its horizon.... Imagine several of these army corps in motion at one time."

Hebron Church (CM)

Corporal James Anderson from Wisconsin recalled that "after we passed Mangohick Church the face of the country changed. It was more open, cleared fields were on every hand, and as we marched through the open country the sun beat down pitilessly upon us." Hotter still were the angry gazes of the citizens. A veteran of the 87th Pennsylvania recalled that "As the army passed through this country of Confederate adherents, the

The Federal pontoon bridge at Nelson's Crossing (LOC)

blinds of the windows in the houses were usually closed and scarcely a person was to be seen. But behind those blinds, scornful and revengeful eyes watched the 'yanks' as they marched to the music of the Union."

Hebron Church stands at the junction of Route 30 and Dabney's Mill Road (Route 604). Take Dabney's Mill Road (Route 604) and follow it for one-half mile. Turn right onto Nelson's Bridge Road and drive 2.2 miles to its intersection of Etna Mills Road (Route 614). Pull over where convenient.

GPS N 37° .455717 W 77° .155964

STOP 15: ETNA MILLS

This intersection used to be known as Hickman's Gatepost. The II and VI corps spent the night of May 27 about two miles to the west, your right. Their march for the Pamunkey commenced about 8:00 o'clock on the morning of May 28, and the first elements reached this intersection soon after. Here they turned south (in the direction you are headed) and relied upon parallel farm roads for the reminder of the three-and-one-half-mile march to Nelson's Crossing on the Pamunkey.

Continue south on Nelson's Bridge Road for 3.7 miles until you see a Civil War Trails marker. Park on the right side of road and carefully cross the road to read the sign. First look behind you at the magnificent white frame home, "Wyoming," on the ridge.

GPS N 37° .431972 W 77° .171090

STOP 16: "WYOMING" (PRIVATE PROPERTY) AND NELSON'S CROSSING

Nelson's Crossing (CM)

Built around 1795, "Wyoming" was named for Pennsylvanians of the Wyoming Valley who were massacred in the Indian raids of the Revolutionary War. The residence was first occupied by George Washington Hoomes and his wife, Martha. In 1839, the Nelson family acquired the property. At the time of the war, Henrietta Nelson, known affectionately as the "widow Nelson," managed the 1,200-acre farm with

Wyoming sits atop a ridge overlooking the broad floodplain of the Pamunkey River. (CM)

her two daughters and several servants. Her son, Pvt. Thomas C. Nelson, rode with the 4th Virginia Cavalry and died in action on June 24, 1864. By May 1864, the home must have fallen into disrepair because Lt. Col. Theodore Lyman of Meade's staff described it as "a large, tumble-down, wooden building, like so many more in Virginia. There were pleasant trees about it," he wrote, "and, at the cold spring, was a beech that, as an enthusiastic soldier remarked was 'a regular Vermonter.'"

As two Union army corps descended on Wyoming from the direction of Mangohick Church, Col. Bradley Johnson of the Confederate army paid a visit to the Nelsons. Colonel Johnson was gathering intelligence about the approaching Federal infantry. He stayed at the house as long as was prudent but was unable to return to check on the Nelson ladies because, as he wrote, "the enemy has a safety guard established at her door."

One half mile ahead of you is the Pamunkey River, described by a Wisconsin soldier as "deep, muddy and the crookedest stream I ever saw." A soldier of the 118th New York remarked that "it has been said of this sinuous river that a steamer going north meets itself going south and exchanges signals to avoid collision."

By the afternoon of May 27, a river crossing had been established at Hanovertown, three miles to the east (your left as you face the river). The weary

Recent rains left the Pamunkey River running high. (CM)

bridge builders of the 50th New York Engineers had little time to rest. Orders arrived from army headquarters at midnight to have a second bridge completed at Nelson's by sunrise. The work began at 6:00 a.m., and in one hour a rickety 146-foot canvas pontoon bridge was in place, approximately 50 yards upriver from the modern bridge. The engineers found themselves short of the prescribed number of pontoons and were forced to expand the intervals between the boats. Despite the bridge's frail appearance, both the infantry and artillery of the VI Corps, which began arriving about 7:30 that morning, passed over without incident. There was some humor in the appearance of the bridges, according to Lyman. "These canvas pontoons are funny looking; they consist of a boat-shaped frame, which is wrapped in a great sheet of canvas and out in the water.... It looks as if the Commander-in-chief had undertaken the washing business on a large scale, and was 'soaking' his soiled clothing."

Later in the afternoon, engineers added a second bridge made of wooden pontoons to expedite the crossing of the II Corps. Both Grant and Meade rode up from Hanovertown to watch the movement of Hancock's veterans. Grant appeared tired, according to one witness. Perhaps the painful effects of the migraine still lingered from the previous day. He said nothing to the men, and they silently continued their march into Hanover County.

To reach the site of Hanovertown (an optional stop), continue south on Nelson's Bridge Road 0.9 mile to River Road (Route 605). Turn left and drive 2.9 miles and park on the left side of the road near the historical signs. This is Stop 17.

GPS N 37° .415029 W 77° .144519

If you prefer to skip Hanovertown, continue south on Nelson's Bridge Road 1.4 miles to Williamsville Road. Turn left and drive one-quarter mile. This is Stop 18.

GPS N 37° .424140 W 77° .181009

Aside from the pontoon bridge at Nelson's Crossing, Federal engineers also constructed one at Hanovertown. (LOC)

STOP 17: HANOVERTOWN (OPTIONAL)

Not to be confused with Hanover Court House, this now-quiet crossroads has seen more than its fair share of history. Established as a port on the Pamunkey River in 1676, it was once a candidate for the state capital. Hanovertown contained only a few buildings, mostly workshops and tobacco warehouses. The site was a Revolutionary War encampment for French forces after the battle of Yorktown in 1781.

Eighty-three years later, elements of the Union army crossed the Pamunkey River here into Hanover County. It is hard to picture, but upwards of 20,000 Union troops marched down these quiet country roads. Throngs of now-free slaves greeted them.

The arrival of the Union army meant the *de facto* emancipation of hundreds of slaves. (LOC)

Captain Edward K. Russell of Wright's staff informed his mother that "wherever we went the darkies in droves with their goods & little ones followed after us . . . . As our trains reached near Hanovertown on the Pamunkey," he wrote, "those who saw it say a most affecting scene took place. 'Twas on the afternoon of Sunday 29th, May & there were a hundred or more 'nigs' of all ages & sexs collected together on the river's bank. They celebrated by singing & prayer their deliverance from slavery. One woman as she looked down upon her baby in her arms said 'Bress de Lor' dey can't sell you.'"

Alfred Waud sketched the Union army as it crossed the Pamunkey. (LOC)

Like many soldiers in the Union army, Russell had had misgivings about emancipation, but his views on the subject had changed. "The freeing of the negro is the natural result of the war & the more I see of it the better it is," he confessed. "It takes away from the South one of their main props in continuing the war. When they are obliged to send some of their fighting strength home to raise crops for those in the Army the sooner will they have to give in."

To return to the Lee vs. Grant Trail, make a U-turn and drive 2.9 miles back to Nelson's Bridge Road. Turn left there and drive half a mile to Williamsville Road (Route 615). Turn left and drive one-quarter mile. Pause along the road, being careful of other traffic.

GPS N 37° .424140 W 77° .181009

Cavalry clashed in this field on May 27 as Federal horsemen continued to clear the way for the Army of the Potomac's advance. (CM)

STOP 18: SITE OF HUNDLEY'S FARM
AND THE MAY 27 CAVALRY ACTION

After crossing the Pamunkey River, the VI Corps, followed by the II Corps, moved forward about a mile, passing through these cleared fields of the Hundley farm. Brigadier General Horatio G. Wright, the VI Corps' commander, established his headquarters nearby before moving to the Pollard plantation, "Williamsville," a short distance to the south.

The day before, on May 27, Brig. Gen. George A. Custer's Michigan cavalry crossed the Pamunkey at Hanovertown (Dabney's Ferry) and then began clearing the Hanover County roads for the VI Corps. Along this road Confederate cavalry scouts displayed token resistance to the Union cavalry, but the fighting quickly intensified with the arrival of a brigade of North Carolina cavalry led by Col. John A. Baker and the 1st Maryland Cavalry (CSA) commanded by Col. Bradley T. Johnson. While the Confederates constructed makeshift breastworks, Custer's men utilized primitive country roads to their advantage. Incorporating Custer's patented wild saber-slashing attacks, his men struck the Confederates from two sides and drove them from the field. This violent albeit brief combat, known also as the battle at Pollard's farm, resulted in relatively few casualties—fewer than 200 for both sides. To Federal cavalry commanders who evaluated this action in context to the recent fight at Yellow Tavern, it appeared that Lee's cavalry had become demoralized and ineffective. Subsequent cavalry clashes at Haw's Shop, Matadequin Creek, and Cold Harbor suggested that they might be right.

Continue straight ahead for 1.1 miles to Studley Woods Drive. Pause at the driveway there but do not enter.

GPS N 37° .415644 W 77° .180869

STOP 19: "WILLIAMSVILLE" (PRIVATE PROPERTY)

This modern road passes the historic entrance to "Williamsville." The estate's ornate gates and luxuriant landscape were remembered by many Union soldiers who passed by here on May 28. A Vermonter in the VI Corps, apparently moved by the

The gates of Williamsville (CM)

juxtaposition of war and the serenity of blooming gardens, wrote: "We approached this place through long avenues, shaded by the magnolia and catalpa and the large egg-shaped flowers of the former, and the clusters of smaller trumpet-shaped blossoms of the other, variegated with yellow and purple, loaded the air with delicious fragrance, and filled the scene with the most tranquil beauty, strangely contrasting with the smell of powder." Officers shouting orders to "dig in" quickly overpowered the soldiers' infatuation with nature.

"Williamsville" was home to one of the Hanover County's wealthiest citizens, Dr. George Pollard, and his four children. Pollard's wife, Mary Todd, had died in 1862. War came to "Williamsville" early and often. Dr. Pollard's son, Harry, recalled that "most of the time during the war our place was in possession of one side or the other." Union raiders in 1862 and 1863 made off with large quantities of food but left the buildings intact. After the cavalry fight of May 27, wounded soldiers from both sides were brought to the house and placed under Dr. Pollard's care. Then, on May 28, Union officers of the II and VI corps established their headquarters on the first floor of the house, forcing the family to take refuge upstairs.

Federal infantry arrived with orders to quickly fortify their position. All materials were fair game. Stables, fences, a carriage house, and even corn cribs were torn down and the materials incorporated into the defenses. When Dr. Pollard realized that the earthworks were to run through the family cemetery, he successfully pleaded to have a curve placed in the defensive line to avoid the graves.

When the time finally arrived to pause and reflect on the past 24 hours, one New York officer wrote: "What with this fine day, the beautiful country, and the getting south of the Pamunkey, everyone is in great spirits this evening. The general notion is that Lee will not make another stand this side of the Chickahominy, if he does not fall back within the outer works of Richmond itself. His army must be growing smaller (we have over 12,000 prisoners), while we are rejoicing now in daily reinforcements. Even I am beginning to think that we may be in Richmond by the 4th of July." To soldiers on the march, estates like Williamsville were welcome refuges from the sights and sounds of war. "This place seems like a paradise tonight, after my bath and good supper," the officer continued. "All is as quiet as if there was no war: the frogs and crickets make the only noise; the fireflies are brilliant by their infinite numbers. One must go through such a three weeks as we have had to know all the luxury of such a spot, such a night, and a good pipe."

Union soldiers rested here on the night of May 28; the next day they would push westward in search of the Lee's army.

Continue 0.4 mile to Chestnut Grove Church, on the left. Park in the church lot with the church on your left.

GPS N 37° .413724 W 77° .180411

STOP 20: CHESTNUT GROVE CHURCH (POSTWAR)

After crossing the Pamunkey River, Grant and Meade deployed the II and VI corps in a line overlooking Crump's Creek. Lee, they assumed, was somewhere between the Union army and Richmond. On the chance that the Confederate army might take the offensive, orders were issued for the II Corps to construct a line running from the settlement of Haw's Shop, a mile to the south (ahead of you), then crossing the road here, and joining the VI Corps line at Williamsville. The V and IX corps, after crossing at Hanovertown, selected an independent position on the high ground off to your right, where they prepared earthworks.

By noon on May 28, Union soldiers could clearly hear the sounds of conflict emanating a few miles to the south. Earlier that morning Grant and Meade had instructed the Union cavalry to ride ahead and reconnoiter for Lee's army. The troopers moved in the direction of Haw's Shop and then rode east for a mile toward Enon Church. They ran headlong into Confederate cavalry just beyond the church. The presence of a strong force of Confederate cavalry indicated that Lee's army was probably nearby.

Continue straight ahead for 1.3 miles to Studley Road (Route 606). Turn left and in 100 yards turn left again into the parking lot at Salem Church. Park near the Civil War Trails marker. The church entrance is on the opposite side of the building.

GPS N 37° .403392 W 77° .173003

STOP 21: SALEM CHURCH AND THE SITE OF HAW'S SHOP

In 1829, Presbyterians erected this church using bricks that local historians suggest were salvaged from abandoned 18th-century Hanovertown warehouses. The simple but elegant country church is well preserved with its original rectangular sanctuary and a second-floor slave gallery at the rear of the church. Mary Haw, a wartime resident of this small community recollected: "On the Sabbath day the church and churchyard would present an

The front of Salem Church faces away from the parking lot where the tour stops. (CM)

While their cavalry battled near Haw's Shop, Federal infantry entrenched and waited out the fight. (LOC)

interesting picture when the fine, silver-mounted coaches, drawn by slick highly bred horses shining in silver-mounted harnesses drove up near the door to deliver their precious load of feminine beauty."

By 1864, the Haw's Shop community consisted of a schoolhouse, some residences that included "Studley," the birthplace of the great patriot orator Patrick Henry, and the abandoned remains of the machine shop owned by John Haw that gave its name to this vicinity. Haw's shop produced milling and farm machinery until 1862, when the equipment was sold to the Tredegar Iron Works in Richmond. The intersection of five roads here, two of which led to Richmond, made the intersection extremely important to the advancing Federals, as it had been to Confederate cavalryman J. E. B. Stuart two years earlier when he led his troopers past the church in his famous ride around McClellan's army.

On the morning of May 28, Brig. Gen. David M. Gregg formed two brigades of Union cavalry, about 3,500 men, in the fields that then surrounded the intersection. Gregg's orders directed that he scout westward from Salem Church following present-day Studley Road. At 10:00 a.m. the column moved forward. Moments later, shots rang out when Union and Confederate cavalry collided a mile ahead, at Enon Church. Preparing for the inevitable, Union medical officers commandeered Salem Church, which soon filled with casualties. The famous Union diarist Theodore Lyman recorded the macabre scene as it appeared both inside and outside the building. "It was not a cheerful place this church. The pulpit and

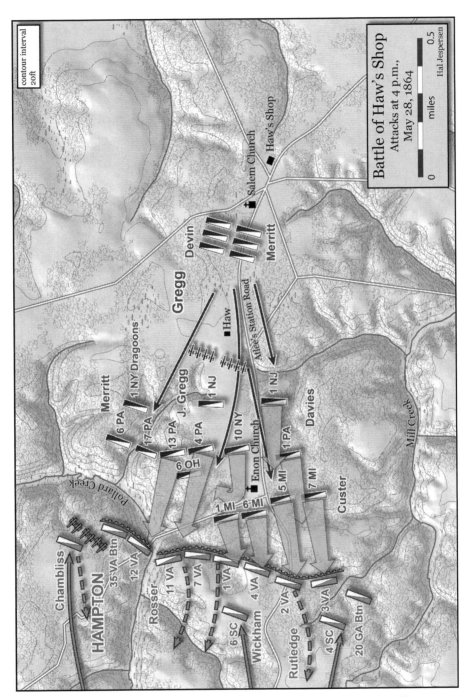

BATTLE OF HAW'S SHOP—Both sides claimed victory in this fierce cavalry action. The troopers largely fought dismounted, and Union cavalry used breech-loading weapons. The Confederates had also recently brought in reinforcements from South Carolina, who fought their first battle here. Late in the day, the arrival of Gen. George A. Custer's Michigan Brigade turned the tide in favor of the Union troopers.

the pews were covered with blood stains and there were a dozen fresh graves outside, [a] sad memorial to the cavalry fight of the day previous."

Salem Church served double duty as a hospital and also as the Union cavalry headquarters. Lieutenant Robert Robertson, who served on the staff of Gen. Nelson Miles, described meeting Philip Sheridan here. "I rode in advance to report the arrival of the brigade to Gen. Sheridan, and seeing a group of cavalry officers eating lunch at the side of an old church I asked for Gen. Sheridan, and was a little surprised when the smallest most ordinary looking man in the party announced himself as the man. After I reported he asked me to dismount and have chicken with them," all this occurring during the height of the Enon Church fighting.

Oak Grove was built in 1792.
(CM)

Return to the intersection you just passed. Proceed through the intersection, going west on Studley Road (Route 606). In one half mile, you will pass the Haw house ("Oak Grove") on your right. This 1792 house (now privately owned) was the home of John Haw III and his wife Mary Watt. It was built in a comfortable style typical for this region: an English basement for refuge in the hot summers and cold winters with a large center hall that divided two rooms on the first and second floors. The Haws had a family of seven: two daughters and five sons. All five sons served in the Confederate army. On the morning of May 28, the remaining Haws were forced to take refuge in their basement. General Gregg and his cavalry entourage reached the Haw house around 10:00 a.m., just after the battle of Enon Church commenced, and promptly established headquarters in a small grove of trees. Union medical officers secured the outbuildings and the upper floors of the house to use as a field hospital.

Proceed one half mile past the Haw house to Enon Church, on the right. Park in the church lot and walk to the Civil War Trails sign. Face in the direction of the Haw house.

GPS N 37° .403495 W 77° .184116

STOP 22: ENON METHODIST CHURCH

As you look back across the field toward the Haw house, it is important to note that the wood lines and fields of the modern landscape reflect almost precisely the area's appearance in 1864. The only missing features are the wooden fences that bordered the roadbed. Enon Church was built in 1837 but burned after the war. Only a portion of the building you see dates from the antebellum period. The obelisk in the churchyard marks the burial location of 27 unidentified Confederate soldiers.

Enon Methodist Church (CM)

Turn around and face west so that Studley Road is on your left and Enon Church is on your right. Around 10:00 a.m. on May 28, the 10th New York Cavalry dismounted in the churchyard and established a battle line that ran perpendicular to the main road. It faced west, the direction you now face. Other troopers were sent ahead around the bend in the road. They hadn't proceeded very far when they encountered the 2nd Virginia Cavalry in advance of Wade Hampton's main Confederate force. The initial clash forced the New Yorkers back to the area around the Haw house, but a vicious Union counterattack led by the 1st Pennsylvania Cavalry erupted into bloody hand-to-hand fighting on horseback. The Confederates fell back a few dozen yards west of Enon Church to a thick woods where the ground rose slightly. There they dismounted and hastily erected fortifications that covered a two-brigade front. "We've got the Yankees where we want them now," Hampton was heard to say.

For nearly eight hours, some of the most desperate cavalry fighting of the entire war evolved from what had been intended as a reconnaissance. At times not more than 200 yards separated the combatants, and in one sector of the fight that distance was reduced to 50 yards. A veteran of the 1st Pennsylvania Cavalry recalled the ferocity of the Haw's Shop combat. "At point blank range the contending parties fought for 7 hours, neither able to carry the other's position, but each determined to hold its own," he wrote. "So rapid and constant was the firing, that during this time the regt, though scarcely 200 of it being engaged expended upward of 18,000 rounds of ammunition. Many of our carbines became so heated as to render them for a time entirely useless."

Quickly, the battle escalated as cavalry reinforcements extended the lines on both sides of the road and artillery units selected the most opportune ground for their business. Individual units were ordered to charge the enemy's defenses hoping for a breakthrough. Not long after arriving on the field, a member of the 10th New York Cavalry felt trepidation at the orders he received to charge into the face of death. "I stood in the midst of the dead and dying while the little missiles battered against the trees and logs and cut the twigs on every side. An aide arrived from General Gregg, saying the line must be advanced. He ducked his head while the bullets whistled past, and shrugged his shoulders as he started for the rear, stating, 'Those are the orders.'"

Private Robert Hubbard of the 3rd Virginia Cavalry wrote his memoir in 1865 while recovering from a wound. His account vividly describes the arrival of the cavalry under Brig. Gen. Williams C. Wickham. These men composed the center of the Confederate position just west of Enon Church. The 3rd Virginia deployed just south of present-day Studley Road. "Wickham's brigade," recalled Hubbard, "in front, came upon the enemy at 12 noon, dismounted, deployed to the right and left, and advancing a little became hotly engaged at once . . . . The woods were thick and we were tolerably well protected . . . . The fire was most incessant and tremendous . . . . Charge after charge was made upon our brigade but to no purpose." The 3rd Virginia Cavalry held its ground for four hours. "A grand charge was made against our whole front," wrote Hubbard. "On, on they came. We had only one thin line and they just swarmed right upon and through the line. Captain Collins and I discharged every barrel of our pistols at a batch of Yankees who got upon the line ten paces to our right and then withdrew . . . . Old Wickham rode around waving his sabre and cursing 'like a trooper,' sure enough."

Wickham restored the line of his overwhelmed Virginians quickly, and soon they were joined by reinforcements from Georgia and South Carolina. The men of the Lowcountry had recently arrived in Richmond and were about to learn a difficult lesson about war, Virginia-style. When they arrived on the battlefield, the South Carolinians discovered a drainage ditch that they immediately occupied for protection. Private Edward Wells of the 4th South Carolina Cavalry described his unit's baptism of fire. "Forward [into the ditch] the men pressed . . . and from there they soon began to make it hot for the enemy, many of whom were as close to them as thirty yards . . . . Most of the shots had to be snaps, fired at faces only for a second thrust from behind a tree, or peering round a bush, or at the rifle flashes, which were sending the lead zipping and singing through the air like devil's bumblebees . . . . Thus the fighting went on, and every moment the boys settled down better and

Twenty-seven unidentified Confederate soldiers rest on the grounds of Enon Church. (BD)

better to their work. After a while someone noticed that bullets were coming in not only from the front but also from the flank. [Lieutenant] Newell could see that his company was being encircled from the left, and springing back to his men, ordered them to save themselves."

Because much of the action was obscured by the smoke and trees, the South Carolinians were unaware that a brigade of Michigan cavalry under Custer had succeeded in flanking their position. They were some of the last remaining Confederate soldiers on the field and were about to be annihilated. Fortunately, quick-thinking officers dashed in among the men and ordered them to the rear, preventing their already high casualty numbers from escalating still further. As a result of their bravery at Enon Church, no longer would the South Carolinians be referred to by their Southern comrades as the "kid glove company."

By the evening of May 28, the cavalry of both sides abandoned the battlefield. The Confederates again crossed Totopotomoy Creek, reporting to Lee that several of the prisoners were Union infantry of the V and VI corps. With this knowledge, the Confederate commander shifted his three corps closer to the Totopotomoy, covering all possible avenues of approach available to Grant. The Federal cavalry turned and rode eastward (behind you), camping in the vicinity of Old Church. They would leave the task of finding Lee's army to the infantry.

The next day, May 29, Maj. Gen. Francis C. Barlow's First Division of the II Corps pushed west through the Haw's Shop battlefield in its pursuit of Lee. A Union officer described the evidence of the recent fight: "[We] found many of the enemy's dead along the road and in the woods to the right, who were killed in the fight yesterday with our cavalry. Some of them evidently just from Richmond by their shining new uniforms and clean shirts, a rarity to our eyes now. The dead officers were particularly noted for their bright uniforms and 'city look.'" The dead soldiers were most likely from the South Carolina regiments who had recently arrived in Richmond and entered the battle with new equipment and fresh spirit.

When you depart Enon Church, continue west on Studley Road (Route 606) for approximately 1.5 miles to Sir Bradley Court, on your left. Pull into the court and turn around.

GPS N 37° .402754 W 77° .195870

STOP 23: UNION ARMY HEADQUARTERS

Around noon on May 30, Grant moved his headquarters to this vicinity. Diarist Lyman recorded this description of the headquarters camp: We were "in a dreary, sandy clearing, with scrub pines about it," he wrote. "Three or four dead rebels were found still hid in the bushes . . . not a tree but had a carbine bullet, I counted five in one within the space of a hat . . . . The weary staff were getting a nap in their tents."

Throughout the afternoon, couriers arrived to update Grant on the army's progress. At 4 o'clock, a message arrived from Meade, who was elsewhere with the army, with information that Sheridan had engaged Confederate cavalry along

Matadequin Creek while reconnoitering the roads to Cold Harbor. Near dusk, Grant notified Meade that Maj. Gen. William F. Smith's XVIII Corps was, at that moment, steaming up the Pamunkey River toward White House Landing. After Smith's 18,000 men debarked, Meade expected them to make a night march to join the army. He feared Lee might attempt to intercept them along the way. As a precaution, Grant directed Meade to insure that Sheridan's troopers were keeping constant vigilance for Confederate activity along the roads emanating from Cold Harbor.

Grant remained in this location until the next day when he moved his headquarters to the Via house, approximately three miles southeast of here.

Turn left and continue west on Studley Road (Route 606) for 0.7 mile. Just past Rural Point Road (Route 643) you will come to Rural Point Elementary School, on your left. Pull into the school lot and park near the Civil War Trails marker that stands near Rural Point Road. Face west toward Studley Road.

GPS N 37° .381902 W 77° .195000

STOP 24: POLLY HUNDLEY'S CORNER AND THE BATTLE OF TOTOPOTOMOY CREEK

Polly Hundley's Corner was the name given to this intersection of four important roads leading to Atlee's Station, Hanover Court House, Mechanicsville, and (indirectly) to Richmond. Records indicate that Polly Hundley had passed away several decades before the Union and Confederate armies arrived here in 1864. A schoolhouse occupied one of the southern corners, possibly near the site of the present elementary school. It was not an uncommon sight to see military forces moving along these roads. In June 1862, Gen. Thomas J. "Stonewall" Jackson's Army of the Valley filed past the intersection on its way to join Lee's forces during the Seven Days campaign. Unlike 1862, the activity here on May 29, 1864, was not transitory; the armies were assembling for action.

On the way here from Enon's Church late in the afternoon of May 29, Gen. Francis Barlow's division of the II Corps encountered a small number of Confederate cavalrymen

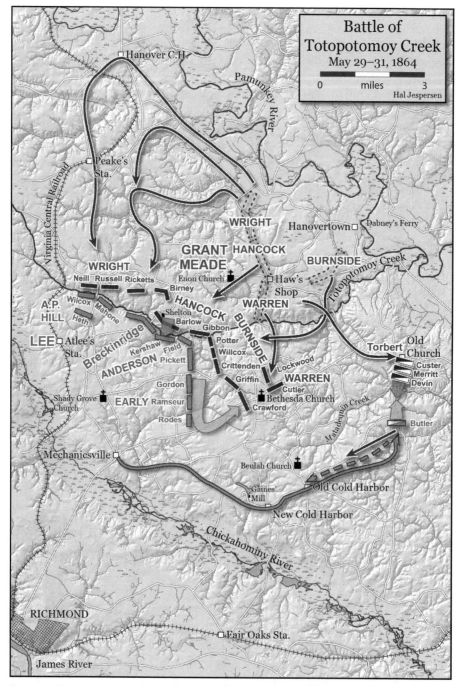

Battle of Totopotomoy Creek
May 29–31, 1864
0   miles   3
Hal Jespersen

BATTLE OF TOTOPOTOMOY CREEK—Using interior lines and good intelligence, Lee managed to deploy the Army of Northern Virginia in a defensive line blocking the roads to Richmond from the east. After skirmishing and probing along the line, notably at Rural Plains, the Army of the Potomac continued to shift to its left. In the meantime, events developed to the southeast that would draw the armies towards the Cold Harbor crossroads.

deployed as skirmishers. The Confederates chose not to resist and fell back through this intersection to the main body of Lee's army, which waited anxiously half a mile to the west, along the banks of Totopotomoy Creek. Local residents told Barlow that there was a division of Confederates entrenched behind the creek. The II Corps continued ahead cautiously with the 26th Michigan in the lead.

To reach Stop 25, exit onto Studley Road (Route 606), turn left, and proceed approximately one-half mile. Turn left into the National Park Service parking lot for Rural Plains and Totopotomoy Creek battlefield.

GPS N 37° .394078 W 77° .204685

STOP 25: RURAL PLAINS AND TOTOPOTOMOY CREEK BATTLEFIELD

The short pathway at this stop leads to "Rural Plains," a ca. 1725 house significant both for its architecture and because of the role that it played as the Union headquarters during the battle of Totopotomoy Creek. At least eight generations of the Shelton family had lived here. The Seven Days campaign in 1862 had come close to the house but had not damaged it. But now, in 1864, the Sheltons found themselves in the crosshairs of the war's two principle armies. When word arrived that the Federal army was moving in their direction, Col. Shelton crossed Totopotomoy Creek into the Confederate lines, presumably to secure protection for his proudly secessionist wife, Sarah, their 15-year-old son, and three daughters. While the

Rural Plains—where Founding Father Patrick Henry married his wife Sarah Shelton in 1754—found itself behind Union lines as the armies squared off along Totopotomoy Creek. (LOC)

Rural Plains, also known as the Shelton house, is open seasonally. The Shelton family lived here until 2006, at which time the National Park Service took over operation of the site. One hundred and twenty-four of the original 1,000 acres remains protected. (CM)

colonel was away, a group of Union officers from the II Corps arrived at the house to see to the family's safety. They politely informed Mrs. Shelton that she and her family would have to relocate. Sarah defiantly told the army ambassadors her opinion of the U.S. Congress, the president, and army of the United States. The exchange ended with Mrs. Shelton refusing to leave and stating that if any injury occurred to her family, responsibility for their blood would rest with the Union officers.

Captain Robert S. Robertson, a staff officer in the II Corps, accompanied the Union troops that deployed around the Shelton home. In his memoir, he recalled the scene: "We halted the line just past the house to reconnoiter the position. Col. Miles, Hallenbeck, Church and myself passed through the large hall to the rear of the house, seeing no one till we got outside where, at the basement door, we found a group of five women and some children, in the greatest conceivable terror, screaming and crying, and frantically beseeching us not to harm them . . . . We succeeded after some time in soothing them with assurances that we would protect them instead of harming them, and got from them the information that it was the house of Mr. Shelton, who was away from home, and that Totopotomay[sic] Creek ran through the ravine just in front of us and a large rebel force was on the other side of it."

In 1864, the vegetative cover was quite different from what it is today. The terrain was largely open and the view from the Shelton house to beyond Totopotomoy Creek was unobstructed. Also. the term "creek" is a misnomer. It consisted of a narrow meandering channel, but it was sluggish, muddy, and in places widened into a nearly impassable swamp. It had extremely high banks all along its course. Except where there were fords or bridges, an army would find it impossible to cross.

Lee's assessment of Grant's intentions was largely correct and his timing was, as usual, impeccable. During the night of May 29, the men of the Army of Northern Virginia fortified the heights for infantry and artillery. When the sun rose the next morning, Union forces on the east side of Totopotomoy Creek saw the imposing Confederate line that had been thrown up along the high ground beyond the creek. It seemed almost like a replay of North Anna.

Once again, Lee had positioned his army in front of Grant and was perfectly situated to protect Richmond and the important railroads. A. P. Hill's Corps formed the Confederate left (north). John C. Breckenridge's division held the center generally following the line of Totopotomoy Creek, while Jubal Early's Corps was positioned on the Confederate right, where it turned abruptly south. (Early had taken over command of the Second Corps from the ailing Richard Ewell on May 27.) Richard Anderson's Corps was held in reserve. Only Confederate skirmishers and a sprinkling of sharpshooters remained on the east side of the swampy bottomland to harass the Union infantry who, by now, were appearing all along their front and digging in.

A two-mile hiking trail winds across the former Shelton property, past an old outbuilding and the family cemetery, and down to the banks of the Totopotomoy. A bridge lets hikers visit the Confederate position, as well. (CM)

On the morning of May 30, the remaining divisions of Hancock's II Corps arrived along the creek and prepared a line of fortifications that extended through the Shelton farm and continued a short distance north of Studley Road. Later that day, the VI Corps extended Hancock's line farther to the north, and the IX Corps formed to Hancock's left, in the vicinity of Polegreen Church. Warren's V Corps held the army's extreme left resting near Bethesda Church. The sandy Hanover soil took much of the back-breaking toil out of digging trenches, but the Confederate infantry fire added considerable danger to the work. Lieutenant Robertson recalled the difficulty of building trenches under fire: "Intrenching tools were brought up and we commenced work, but it was difficult to keep the men at work under the galling fire which the rebels kept up. They would cast up a shovel full of dirt and then lie down in the wheat until the bullets which the throwing up of earth attracted had passed over, then resuming their labor. This delayed the work of intrenching until a bank had been thus raised high enough to afford a partial protection to the working party . . . ."

Several well-preserved sets of Union earthworks are visible along the hiking trail. (CM)

Grant's strategy on the morning of May 30 was to push his line forward to feel Lee's position and search for an opening. In several locations regiments and groups of skirmishers, acting independently, swept towards the creek, and in one instance they succeeded in getting across. If these piecemeal assaults did any good at all, it was in quieting the Confederate skirmishers until Union artillery could be brought up and placed into the line.

All this activity prompted the Confederate artillery to open a cannonade. They directed much of their fire at the Union guns posted near the Shelton house. The Federal artillerists replied to the Confederate guns and brought into action a battery of Coehorn mortars that was positioned almost directly in front of the Shelton house. These short, stubby guns opened an effective counterbattery fire that temporarily silenced the Southern guns. Eventually, however, the Confederates moved their guns out of the range of the mortars and resumed their fire. Lieutenant Robertson remembered the intensity of this long-range Confederate fusillade. "From their new position they recommenced shelling us, and two of their guns were turned on the Shelton house, from the roof of which our Signal officers were taking observations and signaling. They kept up a heavy fire on the house for more than an hour, and it was completely riddled, the women in the basement shivering and almost fainting from terror." About noon, Robertson and some fellow officers sat down in front of the house to eat lunch. Suddenly, he wrote, "a shell came through to the wall and exploded in the room over us, blowing out the windows and filling our lunch basket with broken glass and mortar, effectively ruining our dinner."

A member of the 1st Maryland Infantry (C.S.A.) wrote in his diary about May 30: "Some skirmishing. About 11 A.M. our batteries opened. 12M. Yanks open. They fire high, most of the shells passing over us, we being in a hollow to right of last night's position. A little after sunset Yanks open a heavy fire of shells with spherical case. Have our range well, but fortunately none hurt."

During the cannonade, the Shelton house was reputedly hit 52 times. Some of the damage to the west wall is still visible today. Fifteen-year-old Walter Shelton penned an account of this action, which was recently discovered in the house when the National Park Service acquired the property. Wrote Shelton, "The cannonading was very heavy most of the day & night. The house was struck by a good many shells & and right many exploded in the house when a shell would strike the chimney or near by it the dust & soot would be so great that we could hardly breath. Could not see their hands two inches off. Three shells went through one hole . . . . The officers were very kind to us during the hardest part of the fighting they would send their men in the house when shells exploded to put out the fire."

By the end of the day on May 29, Federals had suffered slightly more than a thousand casualties, Confederates slightly less than that. It was math that the outnumbered Lee could not hope to sustain over time. (CM)

Late in the evening, Union infantry made another attempt to cross the creek. Leading the assault was the 7th New York Heavy Artillery, a unit that had been recently taken from the protection of the Washington defenses and converted to infantry. In a spirited little attack, the men sloshed their way across the creek and succeeded in driving the Confederate defenders from their earthworks. Their success was short lived, as later that night they were recalled back across the Totopotomoy.

Grant continued to probe Lee's Totopotomoy Creek position the following day. The VI Corps

"The cannonading was very heavy most of the day & night. The house was struck by a good many shells . . ." wrote one member of the Shelton family. (CM)

succeeded in getting across the swampy bottomland but was prevented from penetrating any further. Some of the II Corps posted near Shelton's also got across, but a wise veteran soldier remarked, "We very soon discovered that we had no business on that side of the stream, and that if we didn't get back we should arrive in Richmond several days in advance of the army. Our movement to the rear was made with great dash."

Among those participating in these assaults was a young soldier in the 106th Pennsylvania. "Early on the morning of the 31st," he wrote, "crossed the Totopotomoy Creek, drove their skirmishers into their works and kept up a continual heavy skirmishing all day, but gaining no great advantage except a foothold on that side of the creek and to impress the enemy that an attack was threatened."

Nightfall brought an end to the day's largely unproductive fighting. Union casualties along the Totopotomoy since May 29 totaled roughly 1,000, while Lee lost slightly fewer. A "wait and see what your opponent will do next" attitude now seemed to permeate both army commanders. What ended the inaction that evening was information that Union and Confederate cavalry had collided earlier in the day at the Cold Harbor crossroads, eight miles to the southeast. Both sides rushed troops to defend this previously unimportant intersection, setting the stage for the climatic action of the Overland Campaign.

The Rural Plains site is open daily, dawn to dusk, and the house is open at different times throughout the year. After parking your car take a short walk to the kiosk at the trailhead for an orientation to the 18th- and 19th-century story of the site. A free brochure outlines a 1.5-mile walking trail that includes stops at the Shelton house, the family cemetery, and other key locations associated with the battle. When you have finished exploring this site, return to your car and retrace your steps to Rural Point Elementary School. Just beyond the school, turn right onto Rural Point Road (Route 643). Continue 1.6 miles to Heatherwood Drive. Turn left onto Heatherwood Drive and then right into the Polegreen Church parking lot. Walk over to the ghost image of the former church and face west, toward Rural Point Road.

GPS N 37° .384392 W 77° .194793

STOP 26: POLEGREEN CHURCH

A simple yet elegant wooden colonial church stood here when Union and Confederate armies arrived along Totopotomoy Creek in May 1864. More than 100 years earlier, Hanover Presbyterians challenged the only official religion in the colony, the Anglican Church, and won the right to construct four churches in the region to practice their religion. Polegreen was one of those churches. The Reverend Samuel Davies ministered to the early congregation, which included a young Patrick Henry.

Early on May 28, infantry and artillery from Jubal Early's Corps moved into position along this sector of the Totopotomoy Creek battlefield. Their line of earthworks ran roughly parallel to the modern Rural Point Road, approximately one-quarter mile to the west. The Third Richmond Howitzers unlimbered its battery of four guns on a slight rise directly across the field, due west of Polegreen Church, to your left as you face Heatherwood Drive. Confederate pickets dug in all along the Totopotomoy Creek bottom that you passed on your way here.

About 8:00 a.m. on May 31, Union forces of the II Corps received orders to cross the Totopotomoy, one half mile ahead of you, and engage the Confederates. Two brigades of the II Corps found the going easy at first, but after crossing the creek they ran headlong into Confederate skirmishers protected by rifle pits. Tenacious fighting forced the Confederates to withdraw up the hill. The Southerners continued past this position and across the road to the safety of their main line. Some of the Union troops pursued past the church but were stopped by the deadly Confederate artillery and infantry fire that swept the open fields. A member of the 36th Wisconsin recalled the intensity of their "baptism of fire": "The field which we partly crossed had been cultivated. It was very dry and the bullets as they struck the ground would throw up the dust as it does when heavy drops of rain fall on a dusty road."

A Massachusetts soldier remembered the intensity of the Confederate fire and ever-present death on the battlefield. "[Capt.] Mumford was behind a tree, and had just fired his piece when he fell at my feet, shot through the head. All the fire of the rebels was concentrated on this spot. No man could live a moment unless he lay close to the ground. Assisted by one of my sergeants I placed a rubber blanket under the captain and dragged him to the rear . . . . As the firing ceased for a time, we made a rude coffin and laid him to rest. We nailed a wooden slab on the tree, enclosing the grave with a little fence." The II Corps men stopped and entrenched along the edge of the woods, where remnants of their line can be seen today. The IX Corps made little progress after fording the creek and simply dug in.

This action marked the transition between the battles of Totopotomoy Creek and Cold Harbor. While the fighting took place here at Polegreen Church on May 31, a sharp cavalry engagement broke out at the Cold Harbor crossroads. Union cavalry succeeded in holding that strategic intersection, but reports to Union headquarters indicated that Confederate infantry were there as well. If the Confederates broke through at Cold

Harbor, Grant's southern flank would be in jeopardy. The Union commander acted decisively, sending the VI Corps on a night march to Cold Harbor, where it would be joined by the XVIII Corps, which had been sent to Grant as reinforcements from Maj. Gen. Benjamin F. Butler's Army of the James.

During the night of May 31 and into the early dawn of June 1, elements of the Union and

Polegreen Church, destroyed on May 31, 1864, was resurrected in a fashion in 1995. A steel-frame replica conjures the church's original appearance. (BD)

Confederate army began disengaging from their Totopotomoy Creek positions. Just after sunrise on June 1, the Union II Corps was ordered to probe the Confederate line from the Shelton house to a point beyond Polegreen Church. Several Union brigades attempted to reach the Confederate position once again but were stopped by devastating infantry and artillery fire. Word went back to Union headquarters that the Confederate lines in that sector were still held in force. Late in the afternoon, the fighting renewed, but it was largely a dual between opposing artillery. A round from the Richmond Howitzer battery exploded inside Polegreen Church, setting it on fire. In 1995, the Polegreen Church Historical Foundation placed a white steel frame structure above the foundation of the church to replicate its wartime appearance.

Return to Rural Point Road and turn left. Drive south and in one-half mile park in the unimproved pull-off just before you reach the stop sign at Polegreen Road (Route 627). You will be facing south.

GPS N 37° .381902 W 77° .195005

STOP 27: HUNDLEY'S CORNER

The 36th Wisconsin monument sits on the far side of the field from Hundley's Corner. (CM)

This historical intersection, known as Hundley's Corner, was first made famous in 1862. On the evening of June 26, "Stonewall" Jackson halted his division in these open fields and went into camp while the battle of Beaver Dam Creek raged not four miles away. Two years later, on May 28, 1864, the Southern army returned, digging a line of fortifications designed to prevent the Federals from moving west along Pole Green Road, known historically as the Shady Grove Road. At this intersection, the Confederate line created a salient that protruded slightly eastward, giving the Southern gunners command of the open ground in front.

Confederate forces under Richard Anderson occupied these works from May 28–31 but saw little action. On the afternoon of May 31, Anderson's men evacuated these works and went to Cold Harbor. Two brigades under Maj. Gen. Henry

Heth took their place. Late on June 1, as Heth's men were settling in, a wave of Union blue was seen approaching diagonally across the open field to your left. When it got to within 50 yards of the earthworks, Confederate artillery and infantry opened fire, tearing huge gaps in the Union line. The attackers, mostly men from Wisconsin, had two tasks: to see if the Confederates were abandoning their works and to prevent Confederate reinforcements from joining an assault that was then taking place against the Union V Corps north of Bethesda Church. A member of the 36th Wisconsin recalled the ordeal: "The works we charged were about [180 yards] across a cleared field. We made about half the distance when they opened on us with grape and canister—and Oh horror! I never wish to see another charge if they prove as fatal as this."

All of the Union regiments turned back except the 36th Wisconsin. These men struggled to get to the works, and some even made it over the top, where they were captured. Private Charles Storke dropped behind a tree that had been cut down and blazed away until he had no choice but to surrender. "Men were rising around me, their hands in the air. There was nothing else to do; we wouldn't retreat and we couldn't go forward. Thirty-eight of us were taken at that time."

Storke was one of the lucky ones. He was taken to Richmond as a prisoner but survived the war. Of the 240 men that went into the fight with his regiment, 140 were killed, wounded, or captured. After the war, Storke returned to the field where the 36th saw their first combat, and in 1910 he purchased a plot of ground for the purpose of erecting a monument to the valor of his Wisconsin comrades. If you turn to the left, you will see the monument about 400 yards distant along the road.

This concludes the North Anna River portion of your tour. To reach the first stop on the Cold Harbor tour, turn left on Pole Green Road (Route 627). Continue 1.9 miles to the intersection of Walnut Grove Road (Route 615) and turn right. Drive nearly one mile to the Mechanicsville Turnpike (Route 360). Cross the highway and proceed one-quarter mile to First Shiloh Baptist Church on the left. Park at the church and stand so that Walnut Grove Road is on your right.

GPS N 37° .372566 W 77° .175215

Cold Harbor

CHAPTER FOUR
JUNE 1-13, 1864

The potential disaster at North Anna had convinced Grant that the Confederate army was on the ropes, and in the days after, he had looked to exploit that weakness. At Cold Harbor, he thought he had finally found it.

But Grant was mistaken. The Army of Northern Virginia, though numerically weakened by the fighting at Wilderness and Spotsylvania Court House, was hardly down for the count. Far from being demoralized, the army was actually in good spirits, believing with some justice that it had whipped the Federals in both the previous battles. That it had not won an even greater victory on the North Anna River was not due to poor morale but to sickness. As luck would have it, Lee fell ill at the very moment when the Union army was most vulnerable to attack. When the opportunity to spring the trap he had crafted arrived, Lee lay prostrate on his cot muttering, "We must strike them a blow—we must never let them pass us again—we must strike them a blow."

At Cold Harbor, he would do just that.

To reach the first stop on the Cold Harbor portion of the tour, get on I-295 and take Exit 37 toward Tapphannock. This will put you on Route 360 heading northeast. Drive 3.7 miles and turn right on Walnut Grove Road (Route 615). Proceed one-quarter mile to First Shiloh Baptist Church, on your left.

The view from the Confederate position at Cold Harbor looking toward the Union lines. (CM)

GPS N 37° .372566 W 77° .175215

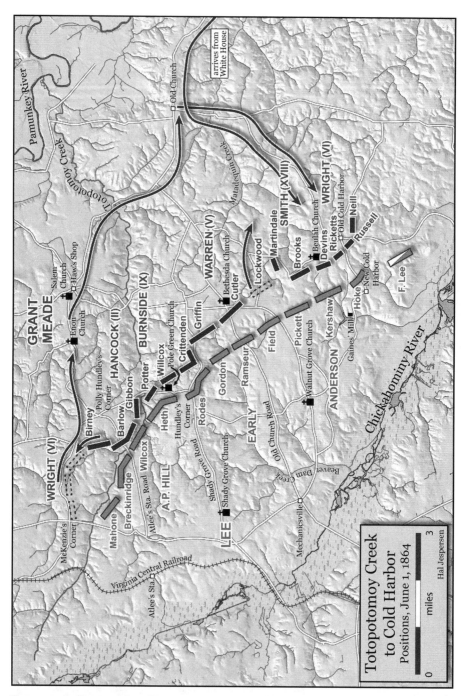

Totopotomoy Creek to Cold Harbor—Delicately, General Wright's VI Corps shifted from the Union army's far right to its far left, arriving at Cold Harbor by the afternoon of June 1. Joining them there was the newly arrived XVIII Corps under General Smith, which had journeyed by water from Bermuda Hundred. Burnside's IX and Warren's V remained near Bethesda Church but shifted positions over the next few days.

STOP 1: BETHESDA CHURCH

Because the Bethesda Church battlefield has been entirely lost to development, it is difficult to both appreciate the scale of combat here or find good stopping points. A great deal of maneuvering and fighting took place here at the end of May and beginning of June 1864. The church itself, now gone, stood east (left) of the modern school you passed at the intersection. You are now facing southwest, in the direction of the Confederates, who attacked toward your position.

A great deal of movement and skirmishing took place here, with the two sides eventually changing positions 360 degrees. On May 30, the Union troops faced south and the Confederates attacked north toward them. By June 3, Union troops were to the south and attacked north towards the Confederates. (LOC)

May 30 was the last day of service for a group of Union veterans: the Pennsylvania Reserves of the V Corps. It would not be a good last day. After moving into position at noon around Old Church Road (Route 360), the lead brigade of Brig. Gen. Samuel W. Crawford's division dug in. Major General Jubal A. Early pushed Maj. Gen. Robert E. Rodes's division forward to attack, and the Confederates swept over the Federals, driving them back in confusion to the church. Always looking for an opportunity to catch the Federal army off guard and strike a blow, Lee hoped to overrun the Union forces here while they were vulnerable.

As so often happens, however, delays spoiled the success. Brigadier General Stephen D. Ramseur's division attacked next, advancing as far as the Federal positions along Shady Grove Church Road (where you were earlier), but Federal artillery stopped the Confederates cold. Lieutenant C. B. Christian of the 49th Virginia wrote: "At each successive fire, great gaps were made in our ranks, but immediately closed up. We crossed that field of carnage and mounted the parapet of the enemy's

The last action of the Pennsylvania Reserves took place just a few miles from their first engagement at Beaver Dam Creek, two years earlier. Just over half of the men re-enlisted, forming the new 190th and 191st Pennsylvania Regiments. (LOC)

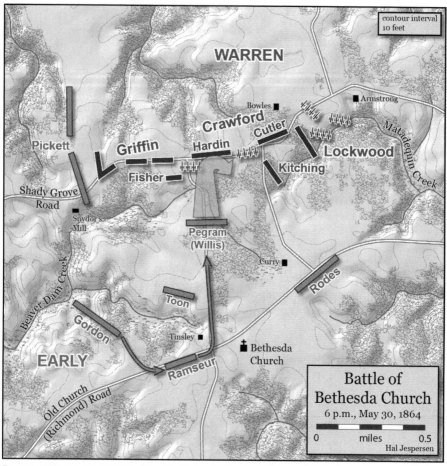

BATTLE OF BETHESDA CHURCH—The Confederate Second Corps assaulted the Federal V Corps, driving them back. Federal artillery fire finally checked the assault.

works and poured a volley in their faces. They gave way but two lines of battle, close in their rear, rose and each delivered a volley into our ranks in rapid succession." The shattered Confederates then fell back to their starting point.

With inconclusive fighting at Totopotomoy Creek (Rural Plains) and Bethesda Church, events were in motion that would draw both armies farther south toward the Cold Harbor crossroads.

Turn right out of the parking lot and drive to the Mechanicsville Turnpike (Route 360). Turn right, drive 3.2 miles, and turn right at the stoplight onto Old Church Road (Route 606). Follow this road 1.3 miles to the village of Old Church. Continue 0.3 mile farther to the parking lot of Immanuel Episcopal Church, on the right.

GPS N 37° .383541 W 77° .125846

STOP 2: OLD CHURCH

This crossroads, named for an 18th-century church (not Immanuel Episcopal), witnessed the passing of the Army of the Potomac in 1862. Major General J. E. B. Stuart's cavalry also passed by here on its June 1862 raid around the Union army. Old Church stood at a vital intersection of roads that ran to New Kent, Hanovertown, Hanover Court House, and Cold Harbor. On May 30, 1864, Union cavalry and infantry moved past the village and turned south, taking the road that ran toward Matadequin Creek.

The church where you now stand was established in 1679. The current building dates back to 1853. It is typical of the many small rural churches scattered throughout eastern Virginia.

Union cavalry passed by the Old Church Hotel on their way to engage the Confederates at Matadequin Creek. (LOC)

Turn left back onto Old Church Road (Route 606) and proceed 0.3 mile to McClellan Road (Route 628). Turn left and follow Route 628 south for a distance of 1.6 miles to Crown Hill Road (Route 632). On the way, you will cross a creek. Immediately thereafter, you will see an old farmhouse on the left as you crest the hill. This is the Liggan house. When your reach Crown Hill Road (Route 632) turn right. Pause here after turning, making sure there is no traffic behind you.

GPS N 37° .371804 W 77° 132938

STOP 3: MATADEQUIN CREEK

You have just driven through the Matedequin Creek battlefield, but the narrow road has no places to pull off. The fighting here and at Cold Harbor reflected the new realities of the armies by 1864. In its first action here was the 7th South Carolina Cavalry, a newly organized unit composed of detachments from across that state combined with a veteran unit. On the Federal side were heavy artillery units, regiments converted to infantry and removed from the Washington and Baltimore defenses to join the army in the field. Both would get their first taste of combat at Cold Harbor.

Matadequin Creek looks much the same today as it did at the time of the battle. (RD)

Here, below Matedequin Creek, Michigan, New York, and Pennsylvania cavalry clashed with South Carolina units, driving them back. The landscape here is still pristine, reflecting wartime conditions. Major General Philip H. Sheridan reported: "The enemy had a very strong position. They were driven

The Liggan house is one of two local homes once used as hospitals during the fighting along Matadequin Creek. (RD)

from it, leaving a number of killed and wounded, 60 or 70 prisoners captured."

Upon cresting the ridge, you saw the Liggan house, on the left. Built about 1853, it was used to treat some of the wounded. Private Oliver H. Middleton of the 4th South Carolina Cavalry, from a prominent Charleston-area family, died here. Oliver was initially buried on the property, but the Middleton family later moved his remains to South Carolina. One of the Liggan sons wrote to Oliver's family: "Just a little while before he became delirious he said, 'Oh! My dear mother if I could only see you once more before I die.'" Having taken down his father's name and address, the Liggans sent word of Middleton's death and burial location to his family.

The building across from the Liggan house, on the right side of the road, is Hill Meadow. It bears bullet holes and bloodstains from the fighting and its later use as a hospital. It was home to the Barker family at the time.

Drive southwest on Crown Hill Road (Route 632) for 3.5 miles and make a sharp right onto Beulah Church Road (Route 633). After two-thirds of a mile, turn right into the parking lot at Beulah Presbyterian Church. Face Beulah Church Road.

GPS N 37° .355801 W 77° .164258

STOP 4: BEULAH CHURCH

While many readers associate Cold Harbor with Union defeat, the opening phases of the battle were Federal victories. It is important to understand this, as it encouraged Grant to keep moving his forces towards the crossroads and eventually led to the ill-fated June 3 attack.

This important landmark, though not the wartime structure, marks the jump-off point for the Union army's June 1 attacks. The XVIII Corps arrived here on the afternoon of June 1 and deployed, with Brig. Gen. John H. Martindale's division advancing across the fields in front of you to engage the Confederates. They gained ground, dug in, and awaited orders for the next assault, which came on June 3.

Look to the north, your right. The white house with the red tin roof in the distance is the David

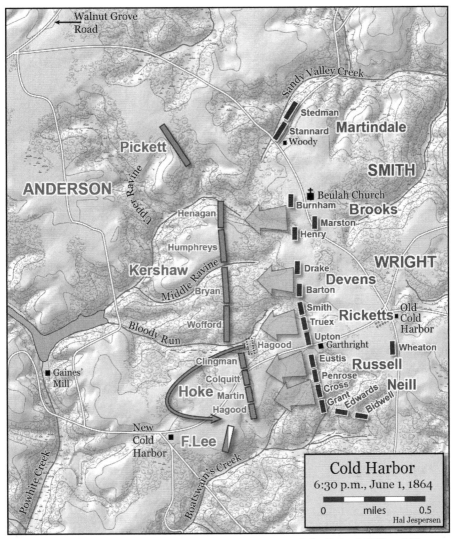

COLD HARBOR, JUNE 1—On the evening of June 1, elements of the Federal XVIII and VI corps attacked Hoke's and Kershaw's Confederate divisions. The success, albeit limited, inspired Grant to follow up with an all-out assault along the entire line the next day, but delays in maneuvering the army into place postponed the attack until June 3.

Woody House (there is debate as to whether this is the original home). When the XVIII Corps arrived here on the afternoon of June 1, Maj. Gen. William F. Smith made the house his headquarters.

From here, as you drive south (left) on Beulah Church Road, you are moving parallel to the Confederate infantry attack on Old Cold Harbor on June 1. To your right, in the open fields, was Col. Lawrence Keitt's brigade of South Carolinians. Recently arrived from his home state with a relatively green regiment, Keitt represented one of the few reinforcements to reach Lee's army that spring. Keitt's regiment, the 20th South Carolina, had more men than the rest of the brigade combined. Observers joked that it was the 20th Corps.

The land across the road from you, to the east, was preserved through the efforts of the Richmond Battlefield Association and the Civil War Trust. Their efforts in the area have saved hundreds of acres, protecting key battle areas from development and allowing public access to previously unseen parts of the battlefields.

Turn left out of the parking lot and retrace your steps south on Beulah Church Road to the intersection of Crown Hill Road (Route 632). Cross the road and pull off to the right into the parking area beyond the intersection.

GPS N 37° .352935 W 77° .161683

STOP 5: OLD COLD HARBOR CROSSROADS

Burnett's Inn gave the crossroads its name. Fighting took place around the intersection on May 31 and June 1. Subsequently, this area was behind Union lines. (LOC)

Probably one of the most misunderstood battles of the war, Cold Harbor has generated many myths. Most visitors to the site do not realize the scale of the battle. The tour will proceed with the armies' preliminary movements, cover the opening clashes, and move on to the main fighting.

You are now at the vital Cold Harbor crossroads, a key point on the battlefield. Neither commander initially sought to occupy this location, but as events developed, it emerged as a key location. Confederate cavalry, driven back from Matedequin Creek, initially tried to hold off their Federal pursuers here. Failing that, they fell back to the west towards New Cold Harbor. Southern infantry began to arrive next and prepared to attack and retake the vital crossroads.

The Union army had successfully crossed the Pamunkey River and maneuvered southeast through Hanover County. The Confederate cavalry had not offered its normally tenacious resistance. Grant was confident, noting that "Lee's army is really whipped. The prisoners we have taken show it and

This open ground witnessed the fighting on May 31 between Torbert's Union cavalry and Hoke's Confederate infantry. On the evening of June 1, Union troops, including the 2nd Connecticut Heavy Artillery, moved right to left to assault Hoke's division. (RD)

the actions of his army shows it unmistakably." That overconfidence was proven wrong at Cold Harbor.

The Union cavalry that occupied the ground dug in, erecting hasty earthworks. These troopers would face Keitt's attack the next day, June 1. Wrote one Maine trooper, "Our position was anything but satisfactory, and we began to dig for our lives." Face north, the direction from which you just came. Keitt's men emerged from the woods ahead of you and faced a devastating fire from the Union troopers here, most of whom had repeating carbines. These weapons, now standard issue for Union cavalry, enabled smaller numbers to effectively hold off larger forces of attackers. Keitt was killed in the effort, and his brigade fell back in confusion.

Later, elements of the VI Corps arrived. The constant movements in the heat had exhausted the men. One wrote that "marching had completely worn us out, and we were so reduced in strength and mental perception that it was a matter of dispute whether we were living or dead." Moving rapidly forward, they deployed and prepared to assault the Confederates to your left-front. Among them, in the front line, was the 2nd Connecticut Heavy Artillery, a green unit. Its commander, Col. Elisha Kellogg, was a veteran and advised his officers before the attack: "Fire not a shot until you are within the enemy's breastworks. I will be with you."

The New Englanders charged and along with the 14th New Jersey broke through the improvised Confederate line. Their success came at a price: Kellogg was killed and his regiment lost 386 of its 1,800 men. As darkness fell, the Confederates withdrew and erected a new line of earthworks, the exhausted Federals consolidating their position in the newly captured line.

Union earthworks, June 1, 1864. The men did not enjoy their stay here. Lt. Col. Theodore Lyman wrote, "It was a Sahara intensified, and was called here Cool Arbor!" (LOC)

Encouraged by the poor performance of the Confederates at Matadequin Creek and at the Old Cold Harbor crossroads, and heartened by the large number of prisoners taken, Grant felt Lee's army to be on the verge of collapse. He ordered a massive assault for dawn the next day. But it took longer than anticipated to get troops into position (the II Corps, for example, had to move from the Union army's extreme right to its far left), forcing Grant to reschedule the attack for dawn, June 3. In the meantime, the Confederates had time to strengthen their position.

As you look out over the fields around you, Union troopers repulsed Keitt's attack to the north. Federal cavalry also dug in to the west, your left, where the ground rises slightly. Unable to reclaim this ground, the Confederates took up a position closer to Richmond, and the Federals prepared to strike them there.

The name for this spot comes from a tavern that stood at the eastern side of the intersection. Because it did not serve hot meals, it was called "Cold Harbor." This intersection saw the passage of armies more than once. In 1862, the Union V Corps under Gen. Fitz John Porter passed by on its way to Mechanicsville, prior to the Seven Days' battles. During the battle of Gaines's Mill, on June 27, 1862, Gen. Stonewall Jackson's corps launched assaults directly to the south against Porter's men. Going back even further, Continental troops passed here in 1781 during the British invasion of Virginia.

Burnett's Inn, a small, unassuming landmark, saw the passage of armies in 1781, 1862, and 1864. (LOC)

Turn right out of the parking area and immediately turn right again onto Cold Harbor Road (Route 156). In one mile, turn right into the National Park's Cold Harbor Battlefield unit. Park at the visitor center and face the park tour road.

GPS N 37° .350772 W 77° .171303

STOP 6: COLD HARBOR VISITOR CENTER

The visitor center at this stop has public restrooms and exhibits about the fighting at Cold Harbor. Staffed daily, rangers are on hand to answer questions and orient visitors. Here, the National Park preserves just a one-mile-long, 180-acre section of what was a seven-mile-long front. This area saw fighting on June 1, 1864, but only

some of the bloody June 3 action is preserved here, much of the heaviest combat taking place on the private property above and below the park.

If time allows, take the one-mile walking trail that begins here. This trail highlights the successful June 1 Union attack that broke the Confederate line to the east, ahead of you in the distant tree line. Along the way are some well-preserved earthworks from the Confederates' second line. If you prefer, take the extended trail, which will add just over a mile to the walk. The extended trail passes through more excellent trenches, and includes some of the June 3 battlefield.

Before leaving the visitor center area, walk to the pair of cannons beyond the building and face east, the direction the guns are pointing. You are currently behind the Confederate line of June 3. On June 1, North Carolina troops occupied a hastily dug line in the woods 400 yards in front of you, across the field. This line was broken by the 2nd Connecticut Heavy Artillery and other units that evening. The Southerners then fell back here and constructed a new line of trenches. The earthworks are now gone, but they ran along the edge of high grass in front of you. If you look over your left shoulder, beyond the park tour road and the road signs in the distance, you may be able to see a surviving portion of the line that ran through here. It continued across your front and to your right, crossing the road onto the private property to the south, where modern houses now stand.

The Cold Harbor Visitor Center (top) features exhibits and orientation, a one-mile walking trail with some exceptionally preserved earthworks (above), and artillery pieces behind the building (below). (CM)

On June 3, Pennsylvania troops across the field from you, occupying the captured Confederate line, refused to charge. Such disobedience was not

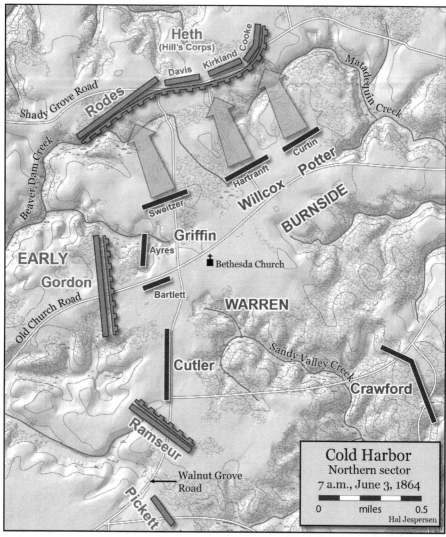

Cold Harbor, June 3, Northern Sector—By June 3, the Federal and Confederate positions in the northern sector of the battlefield near Bethesda Church had reversed. When Grant ordered his all-out assault that day, his IX Corps attacked from the old Confederate positions northward toward A.P. Hill's new lines. Compare this map to the troop positions on May 30 (pg. 138).

uncommon that morning, and the men suffered no repercussions. By contrast, some newer troops with less experience charged with enthusiasm. Look to the right, south across Cold Harbor Road (Route 156), to the open field on the other side. The 8th New York Heavy Artillery charged across that field, its commander, Col. Peter Porter, falling dead not far from the Confederate earthworks. Sergeant Leroy Williams brought Porter's body back to safety, earning the Medal of Honor for

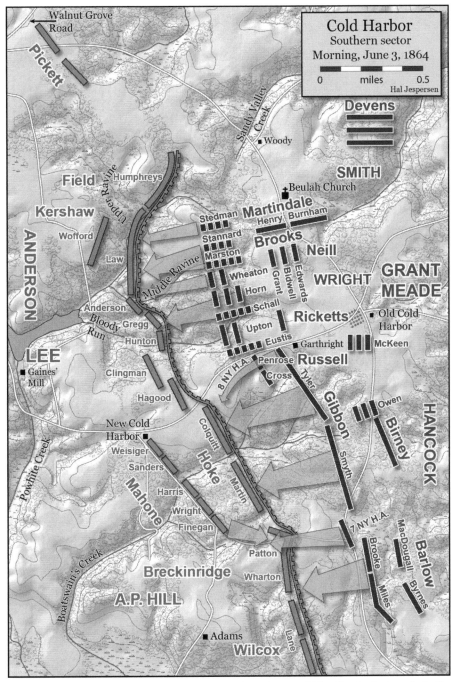

Cold Harbor
Southern sector
Morning, June 3, 1864

0   miles   0.5
Hal Jespersen

COLD HARBOR, JUNE 3, SOUTHERN SECTOR—When Grant launched his all-out attack early in the morning of June 3, disjointed attacks by the II, VI, and XVIII Corps were easily repulsed. A brief breakthrough occurred along Breckinridge's line, but the tide was soon stemmed. "I have always regretted that the last assault at Cold Harbor was ever made," Grant famously wrote in his memoirs. "No advantage whatever was gained to compensate for the heavy loss we sustained."

Grant sits at his Cold Harbor HQ. Tension and friction permeated the atmosphere of Union headquarters, contributing to the uncoordinated attacks of June 3. (LOC)

his actions. The New York regiment lost 475 of its 1,500 men. Wrote one member of the unit: "It was horrible. It is only a wonder that a single man escaped the hail storm of bullets and shell." Heavy artillery units, fighting as infantry, lost as disproportionate a number of men at Cold Harbor as they had at Spotsylvania.

When ready, return to your car and drive the National Park Service tour road. There are three stops on the road.

The park tour road is a two-mile, one-way loop road. From the visitor center enter the tour road and proceed to the first stop, a section of Confederate trenches.

STOP 7: CONFEDERATE TRENCHES

The earthworks you see here were held by Brig. Gen. George T. Anderson's Georgians on June 3. The terrain is similar to that of June 1864: open woods with scattered mature trees. This is one of the best views of the battlefield and gives a feel for the area's wartime appearance. Most of the battlefield within the park is heavily wooded with non-historic trees, and outside the park there is suburban housing.

From here, Anderson's troops poured a deadly fire into the oncoming Union troops. Brigadier General Evander M. Law, who witnessed the attacks near here, wrote: "I had seen the dreadful carnage in front of Marye's Heights at Fredericksburg, and on the old Railroad cut at Second Manassas, but I had seen nothing to exceed this. It was not war, it was murder."

Just above your location, to your left, were men under the command of Col. William Oates of the 15th Alabama. He observed the intensity of the Confederate rifle fire, noting: "I could see dust fog out of a man's clothing in two or three places at once where as many balls would strike him at the same moment."

Because Grant's attack was delayed until June 3, Confederate troops had ample time to dig in. Their lines were angled to catch attackers in a crossfire and took advantage of the open ground the Federals had to cross. You will see the Union soldiers' perspective at the next stop.

Continue on the tour road to the next pullout. Stand facing the marker.

Confederates built elaborate defenses that provided optimum protection while enhancing their firepower by creating fields of converging fire. (RD)

STOP 8: UNION ATTACK

With most of the battlefield unpreserved, this is one of the few locations where you can stand at the site of some of the worst of the Cold Harbor combat. Charging through this area was the Star Brigade of the XVIII Corps, consisting of the 23rd, 25th, and 27th Massachusetts, and the 55th Pennsylvania. The Bay State men suffered terribly here. Their attack originated from near Beulah Church, which you saw earlier. It is to the east, behind you.

The New England troops overran the Confederate pickets but could not reach the main Confederate line. Well-directed enemy fire stopped them cold, and men dropped to the ground for safety. A soldier from the 27th Massachusetts wrote that as they sought cover on the ground, "It was

Here the Georgians of Gen. Anderson's brigade stopped the attacking Federals of the 22nd, 25th, and 27th Massachusetts. The terrain here closely resembles the original 1864 landscape. (RD)

Federals crossed this killing field during the fateful June 3 attack. (CM)

almost impossible to move and live, the lifting of a head or hand being a signal for volleys of musketry." The 27th's commander wrote that his troops "were met by a storm of bullets, shot, and shell that no human power could withstand. Checked . . . and with two-thirds of their number killed or disabled . . . with their hands and tin cups, rifle-pits were constructed. . . . ."

So many men fell that survivors thought the line had been ordered to lie down. Private William Derby of the 27th wrote that "the surface of the field seemed like a boiling cauldron," a result of the impact of dirt flying up from incoming shots. Another soldier from the 25th Massachusetts recalled that "we couldn't retreat without being killed."

Notice the small, hastily dug trenches on the rise 50 yards to the right of the marker. This small line runs parallel to the road and ends before the pulloff where you now stand. Constructed with tin cups, bayonets, and bare hands, it reflects the desperation of those caught here. As you drive toward the next stop, you will see better earthworks, where the men had more time to dig in.

This area closely resembles the 1864 landscape. Note the open forest with the grassy field. There was little cover for the attacking Federal troops other than the slight undulations of the ground.

Continue on the tour road to the next pullout.

As the days went on, both sides dug in and their trenches became more elaborate. One soldier wrote that they lived like gophers. (LOC)

STOP 9: 2ND CONNECTICUT HEAVY ARTILLERY MONUMENT

The newly arrived men from Litchfield County, Connecticut, were eager to prove themselves. The only monument on the battlefield is dedicated to the 2nd Connecticut Heavy Artillery, which attacked through this area on June 1. Just ahead, the trail enters the ravine where Col. Elisha Kellogg was mortally wounded. Brigadier General Thomas L. Clingman, in line with the 51st North Carolina, wrote of "a tall and uncommonly fine looking officer in the front rank of the enemy's column . . . ." He was probably referring to Colonel Kellogg.

The 2nd Connecticut Heavy Artillery was about to experience its first battle, having served in the defense of Washington for most of its existence. It joined the Army of the Potomac on May 20. It was slated to lead the Union attack, and the inexperienced troops went in with enthusiasm. In the fighting the unit lost 386 men, three percent of the male population of Litchfield County. Yet they broke through and took many prisoners. Remember that this action on June 1 was a Union success and encouraged Grant to continue the attacks, resulting in the massive, but poorly coordinated, assaults on June 3.

Dedicated to the men of the 2nd Connecticut Heavy Artillery in their first battle, a monument stands near the location where the New Englanders broke through the Confederate line. (RD)

Starting near the crossroads where you were at Stop 5, the unit attacked west to this position. Above and below them other Union troops advanced in a parallel line. If you choose, walk down the path a short distance to enter the ravine that the New

England soldiers reached in their attack. Just yards from the Confederate trench, they stalled here before sweeping forward to overrun the enemy line. In the swampy ground to the right, troops from New Jersey also broke through, pushing the Confederates back.

Proceed to the end of the park tour road and cautiously turn left onto Cold Harbor Road (Route 156). Traffic can be heavy and moves quickly. Drive just over a half a mile and turn right into the entrance to the county battlefield park and Garthright house.

GPS N 37° .352062 W 77° .164277

STOP 10: COLD HARBOR BATTLEFIELD PARK (HANOVER COUNTY) & NATIONAL CEMETERY

Union troops swept past the home of Miles and Margaret Garthwright on the evening of June 1. This is the only wartime structure accessible to the public on the battlefield. (RD)

There are three sites to see at this stop: the county park, the Garthright house, and the national cemetery. The county battlefield park, which has several walking trails, preserves several good examples of Union earthworks and rifle pits. If time allows, walk the trail to see more of the battlefield. The men in this area were from the II and VI corps. When finished here, walk over to the national cemetery. Losses for the two-week battle were about 13,000 Federal and nearly 5,000 Confederate soldiers.

Although not open to the public, the Garthwright house stands as a witness to the fierce fighting of June 1864. This is one of the few original wartime houses left in the area.

After the failure of the Union attacks on June 3, the armies settled in for trench warfare, digging extensively. Men had to keep their heads down and suffered terribly from heat, thirst, and miserable conditions. For a total of 12 days the two armies sparred at Cold Harbor. The longer the men stayed, the more they dug in, like "prairie dogs," according to one Union private. Life in the trenches was miserable. Union Maj. Gen. Gouverneur K. Warren noted, "The men need some rest." In the trenches, he noted, they were beset by "night alarms, day attacks, hunger, thirst, supreme weariness, vermin, squalor, filth, disgusting odors everywhere."

After the failure of the June 3 attacks, Federal troops dug in—using everything from shovels to bayonets to canteens and tin cups. (LOC)

After some negotiating, Lee and Grant settled on a truce on June 7 to gather the wounded between the lines, most of whom had now died. The loss of so many men from exposure and lack of care is one of the most regrettable events of the war.

Grant saw the futility of further attacks here and prepared once again to move to the left. All along he insisted that his goal was to take the army across the James River, and he began to put that plan into effect. On June 12, the Union army began the difficult process of disengaging from the Confederates and evacuating the Cold Harbor trenches. Staff officer Theodore Lyman noted, "After a stay of 9 days, in this sand field, we broke camp . . . ." The army began moving south, towards the James River. Grant once again completed a successful maneuver under difficult circumstances.

As before, the armies had to make the best of the area's limited road network. Correspondent Charles Page noted that "When a great army moves, it fills all the roads. It seeks every country cross-road, every farm by-road and uses it, no matter how circuitous the road, no matter what direction it pursues, so that it intersects some road that does make toward the point, it must be used."

Across the road from the county park is Cold Harbor National Cemetery. Parking space is very limited, so it is best to walk there. Established in 1866, the cemetery holds the remains of 2,000 Union soldiers gathered from surrounding battlefields, including the 1862 Seven Days' battles.

Interestingly, the veterans placed no monuments on the Cold Harbor battlefield but erected two in the cemetery. Visitors

Cold Harbor National Cemetery holds the remains of two thousand Union soldiers. (RD)

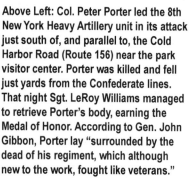

Above Left: Col. Peter Porter led the 8th New York Heavy Artillery unit in its attack just south of, and parallel to, the Cold Harbor Road (Route 156) near the park visitor center. Porter was killed and fell just yards from the Confederate lines. That night Sgt. LeRoy Williams managed to retrieve Porter's body, earning the Medal of Honor. According to Gen. John Gibbon, Porter lay "surrounded by the dead of his regiment, which although new to the work, fought like veterans." **Above Right:** The Pennsylvania monument is dedicated to all the troops from the Keystone State. It lists the state's various units on the back side. **Right:** Prominently located in the Cold Harbor National Cemetery, this monument marks the remains of 889 unknown soldiers. (RD)

will find a monument to Pennsylvania troops there as well as one honoring the 8th New York Heavy Artillery regiment. In the back is an impressive monument, the Tomb of the Unknown Soldier, honoring 889 unknown men buried on either side of it. From there return to your vehicle and resume the tour.

Turn right onto Route 156 and follow it half a mile back to the Old Cold Harbor intersection, where you were earlier. At that point, turn sharply to the right, remaining on Route 156 for approximately one mile, when you will begin to ascend a hill. Just past Old Quaker Road, on the right, look for a low line of Union earthworks that cross the road near the crest of the hill and then run parallel to the road on the left. These are Union trenches constructed after the June 3 assault. Continue on Route 156 for another 0.9 mile and watch for a state

Artist Alfred Waud sketched "The Bucktail's last shot" on June 8. Even though June 3 would see the last major assault, the bloodshed continued for days afterward. (LOC)

historic marker on your right. When you see it, turn right into Turkey Hollow Place and pull off the road.

GPS N 37° .335733 W 77° .155811

STOP 11: FLAG OF TRUCE

Although you are well beyond the park boundary, you are still on the battlefield, which covered a much larger area than what is preserved for the public. As your vehicle is now oriented, Confederate trenches stood in the distance to your right, and Union lines were to your left. Cold Harbor Road, behind you, was in the no-man's land between them.

Near here, Union and Confederate officers met on June 5 to begin the process of a cease-fire. (RD)

The flag of truce at Cold Harbor remains one of the most controversial incidents of Grant's military career. Thousands of wounded men—most of them Union—lay between the lines following the June 3 assault, exposed to the sun. Soldiers on both sides listened to their cries but were unable to succor them.

On June 5, Grant had aide Lt. Col. Theodore Lyman take a letter over to Confederate lines asking for a cease-fire so that both sides could gather the wounded. Lyman carefully made his way from the army headquarters to the II Corps front in this vicinity. Using a torn pillowcase for a white flag, Lyman cautiously worked his way up to the front line, avoiding the ever-watchful sharpshooters. Here, along the road, he met Maj. Thomas Wooten of the 14th North Carolina, commanding the Confederate picket line. Upon learning that an answer would take time, Wooten and Lyman shook hands and parted, agreeing to meet again the next day.

In the meantime, Grant's message made its way

The men of the II Corps made the only breakthrough on June 3, though a fierce counterattack by newly arrived Florida troops and Maryland veterans drove them back. (LOC)

back to Lee's headquarters, near Gaines' Mill. Grant's letter proposed that parties be allowed between the lines to tend to the dead and wounded in areas where no fighting was currently going on. Lee replied that Grant should formally request a flag of truce "as is customary." The understanding was that the commander who asked for a flag of truce admitted defeat. Grant's next letter to Lee on June 6 restated his intention, explaining that the parties going between the lines could carry a white flag of truce.

Lee's reply left no room for further misunderstanding: "I regret to find that I did not make myself understood. When either party desire such permission it shall be asked for by flag of truce in the usual way. Until I receive such a proposition from you on the subject to which I can accede with propriety, I have directed any parties you may send under white flags as mentioned in your letter to be turned back." Grant then replied with a formal request.

Finally on Tuesday morning, June 7, a full four days after the failed assault, the two sides reached an agreement. In his last letter, Grant noted, "all my efforts for alleviating the sufferings of wounded men left upon the battle-field have been rendered nugatory." Lee had agreed to a truce between 6:00 and 8:00 p.m., but his response did not reach Union headquarters until 5:30, making it almost too late to implement. Grant quickly replied, "I will avail myself of your offer at the earliest possible moment, which I hope will not be much after that hour."

That evening the firing stopped and men of both

sides cautiously crept forward to rescue what few wounded soldiers remained and to bury the dead. During this lull men exchanged newspapers, tobacco, and food. Wrote Capt. Asa W. Bartlett of the 12th New Hampshire, "For ordering the charge, or ever allowing it to be made at the time and place it was, there may perhaps be found, among all the surrounding circumstances, some show of excuse, if not justification, but for permitting wounded heroes of that charge to suffer and die as they did, one must search in vain for either." Historians still debate the actions of Lee and Grant in negotiating the truce.

Following this brief respite, the deadly routine of trench warfare resumed. For those in the lines, it was a miserable existence. One Georgian wrote: "It has been raining this evening. Laying in the trenches is very hard work, particularly in the rain. We have been on the front lines four nights, and as the enemy has works in 300 yards of us the men can get very little sleep at night. Going to the spring to get water is a dangerous business." Confederate Gen. E. P. Alexander noted, "We now entered upon 8 days of life in the trenches, which I think were almost the 8 days of greatest hardship that the army ever endured."

When the Union army pulled out on June 12, the Confederates were caught totally off guard. The remainder of the tour follows the Union army as it moved south, towards the James River.

A. DuBois of the 7th New York Heavy Artillery wrote of the Confederate counterattack, "Green soldiers though we were, our short experience had taught us to know just when to run, and run we did, I assure you." Florida and Maryland had few troops with the Army of Northern Virginia, but they distinguished themselves here. One Marylander recalled, "The conflict was brief but terrible. It was hand to hand." (LOC)

Turn around and return to Route 156. Turn right, drive for three-quarters of a mile, and turn left on Market Road (Route 630). In 0.8 mile bear right onto Fox Hunter Lane

(Route 613). Continue for 2.5 miles and bear right again onto Dispatch Road (also Route 613). In 1.3 miles you will come to a set of railroad tracks. There is nowhere to stop here, but you may wish to pause if there are no cars following you. If there are, read the following text at Stop 13.

GPS N 37° .315269 W 77° .115245

STOP 12: DISPATCH STATION

You are now at the site of Dispatch Station, an important landmark in the Seven Days campaign. Grant, Meade, and their staffs camped at the Moody house near the station on the evening of June 12. Lieutenant Colonel Theodore Lyman of Meade's staff wrote that "Moody's is a little house, as it were on skids, like a corn-barn, and with several pleasant catalpas around it." General Grant was found napping on a board.

The march from Cold Harbor was yet another trying experience for the men. Union Gen. Andrew Humphreys wrote that it was "long and exhausting." Colonel Horace Porter of Grant's staff noted, "Although there was moonlight, the dust rose in such dense clouds that it was difficult to see more than a short distance, and the march was exceedingly tedious and uncomfortable." The private soldiers agreed, one recalling that "It was bright moonlight, and the utmost caution was observed that the enemy should not discover their intentions." As you pause here, imagine thousands of weary men trudging along this dusty road through the moonlight.

Continue 1.1 miles to the end of the road and turn left onto Route 249. Drive 0.8 mile to Henpeck Road (Route 665) and follow it 2.8 miles to the Old Roxbury Road (Route 640). Turn right and drive 1.2 miles to Route 60. Also known as the Old Williamsburg Road, Route 60 was the road used by both British and American troops marching to Yorktown in 1781. Turn left onto Route 60 and then make your first right onto Roxbury Road (Route 106). In 0.4 mile look for a Civil War Trails marker and pull into the parking area on the left side of the road. Face in the direction you've been driving.

GPS N 37° .283601 W 77° .080591

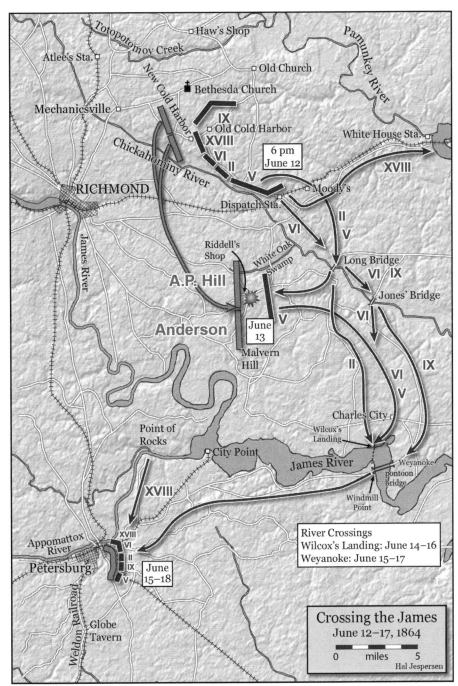

CROSSING THE JAMES—As early as June 5, Grant had decided to move the army south to cross the James River. Two aides, Lt. Col. Cyrus Comstock and Lt. Col. Horace Porter, scouted crossing points and routes of evacuation. The complicated movement was kept secret until June 11, and the withdrawal began the next evening. It went smoothly, and Confederates woke on June 13 to find the Union lines abandoned. The withdrawal went in phases, with troops pulling back to a constricted line while the rest of the army moved southeast. The V Corps then moved to the Glendale area to protect the rest of the army while it crossed.

STOP 13: LONG BRIDGE

The Union army moved south and east along several routes towards an obstacle that had confronted them two years earlier: the Chickahominy River. Weary men shouldered their rifles and secured their gear as they marched along the narrow roads towards their assigned crossings. The dust was horrible as men marched through this area. One-half mile ahead of you was Long Bridge. By 1864 the bridge had been destroyed, and upon

The wide, swampy approaches to the bridge required engineers to construct corduroy roads on either side. Laying down logs allowed men, vehicles, and horses to pass over the wet ground on either side of the bridge. (LOC)

their arrival Union engineers set to work building a pontoon bridge at the crossing. Confederate cavalry on the southern shore harassed the engineers, slowing their work. Eventually Union troopers waded across the swampy river upstream, to your right, and drove the Confederates away.

Major George Ford, the engineer in charge of the bridge construction, noted that "the river was filled with sunken piles and timber, the available passage was very narrow, the debris of the old bridge had to be cleared away, and the abutments cut down." The pontoon bridge ended up being more than 160 feet long.

Brigadier General Charles Wainwright recalled: "The troops were bivouacked a little beyond the bridge, leaving room for the train to be parked between them and the river. . . . We next chose a big tree for our cover, had a fire made, stationed a guard, and stretched ourselves out for a nap." The VI and IX corps crossed farther to the east, your left, at Jones's Bridge, and marched south via Charles City Court House to reach Wilcox's Landing, using what is today Route 155.

Recalling his experience from the Seven Days' battles, a soldier in VI Corps noted, "Two years before, we had crossed the same stream not far from this very spot. . . ." No doubt he and his comrades wondered if this time the results would be different.

Confederate Gen. E.P. Alexander observed of the Union army's movement: "Not only was this strategy brilliant in conception, for which all the credit, I believe, belongs to Gen. Grant, but the orders & the details of such a rapid movement of so mighty an army, with all its immense trains & its artillery, across two rivers, on its own pontoon bridges, make it also the most brilliant piece of logistics of the war."

The next stop, Glendale, is optional. If you wish to go there, continue south on Route 106 for 1.1 miles and turn right onto the Charles City Road, heading west. (This road will later become Route 156.) Stay on this road for 5.7 miles until you reach the Glendale intersection. Turn right at the intersection and immediately pull off the road in front of the stone marker and iron plaque that you find there. Face west, toward Richmond, so that the intersection is on your left.

GPS N 37° .264567 W 77° .135994

If you wish to skip Glendale and jump ahead to Stop 15, continue south on Route 106 for 0.9 mile and turn left onto Barnett's Road (Route 609). Drive 10 miles until you reach Route 5. Turn left and drive 3.5 miles, turning right into Lawrence Lewis, Jr. Park when you see the Civil War Trails marker. Drive to the wharf at the end of the road.

GPS N 37° .190224 W 77° .055258

STOP 14: GLENDALE (OPTIONAL)

You are now at the center of the 1862 Glendale/Fraser's Farm battlefield. The site was also known as Riddell's Shop. In 1864, Union cavalry arrived here and dug in, facing west, towards Richmond—the same direction you're facing now. The cavalry played an important role, screening the movement of the rest of the army and allowing it to cross the Chickahominy and move south to the James River unmolested.

The Union troopers occupied an area stretching from the Charles City Road, to your right, and arcing down to the Willis Church Road, to your left. General Lee sensed the importance of the crossroads and put Southern infantry in motion from Cold Harbor to reclaim it.

On June 13, Maj. Gen. Cadmus M. Wilcox's Confederate division attacked but failed to break through the Union lines here. By evening, Brig. Gen. William Mahone's division moved up on

Wilcox's right, extending the Confederate position down to Willis Church Road. Both sides dug in. At midnight, the Union troopers pulled out, having successfully kept the Confederates at arm's length while the army crossed the Chickahominy.

Wilcox's attack here at Glendale marked some of the last fighting of the campaign. In the six weeks of fighting between the Rapidan and James Rivers, the Union army lost 55,000 men and the Confederates an estimated 33,000, giving the Overland Campaign the sanguinary distinction of being the bloodiest campaign of the war.

Proceed 150 yards up the road, where there is an exit lane. Carefully turn around and return to this intersection. Turn left onto the Charles City Road (Route 156) and drive 1.2 miles to a fork in the road. Take the right-hand fork, continuing straight on the Charles City Road. Drive 4.5 miles farther to Roxbury Road (Route 106). You are now back in the area of Long Bridge. Take a left onto Roxbury Road, cross the railroad tracks, and then take your first right onto Barnett's Road (Route 609). Drive 10 miles until you reach the John Tyler Memorial Highway (Route 5). Turn left and drive 3.5 miles, turning right into Lawrence Lewis, Jr. Park when you see the Civil War Trails marker. Drive to the wharf at the end of the road.

GPS N 37° .190224 W 77° .055258

INTERLUDE: GRAVEL HILL: AN AFRICAN-AMERICAN COMMUNITY CAUGHT IN THE VORTEX (OPTIONAL)

The former site of Gravel Hill, an African-American community impacted by the Overland Campaign, is just a short drive from Glendale. (RD)

Just east of Glendale is Gravel Hill, a community descended from free African-Americans who resided here during the Civil War.

John Pleasants, a local Quaker, freed his slaves in his will in 1771. Pleasants also donated land and money to the families. This action met with opposition, but John Marshall—later the first chief justice of the Supreme Court—successfully argued the case before the Virginia High Court of Appeals. Gravel Hill became one of the few free African-American communities in antebellum Virginia.

During the June 1862 battle of Glendale, fighting raged across the property of Richard and Isaac Sykes, two brothers whose farms sat along Long Bridge Road.

Two years later, members of the community suffered again when the armies skirmished here in June 1864, as well as later during the Deep Bottom and Fussell's Mill engagements of July and August. William James suffered so much loss that he fled with his family to City Point, where he worked for the Union army's quartermaster department.

After the war, many residents filed claims, noting damage such as acres of potatoes, corn, onions, and cabbage trampled or stolen; fences torn down; houses struck by shot and shell; and livestock taken. Still, they rebuilt—and they prospered. In 1866, residents established the Gravel Hill Baptist Church. The modern church building now occupies the same site. Philadelphia Quaker Anna Jeanes helped fund a one-room school here in the postwar years. In the 1930s, a brick school was built to educate the area's African American children. Operating until 1955, it now is a community center with exhibits on the history of Gravel Hill (open by appointment only).

Gravel Hill Baptist Church sits on the site of the community's original church. The church offers more information about Gravel Hill's history at http://gravelhillbaptistchurch.com/about_us1. (RD)

To see Gravel Hill, continue east from Glendale on one-half mile on Darbytown Road and turn left onto Long Bridge Road. In one mile you will intersect with Carter's Mill Road. Gravel Hill Baptist Church will be on the right, and the community center on the left. When finished here, return to Glendale to continue the tour.

GPS N 37° .26206 W 77° .15348

STOP 15: WILCOX'S LANDING

You are now at Wilcox's Landing on the James River. The II and V corps crossed the river at this point, while the VI and IX corps passed over at Weyanoke, just downstream to your left front. To span the river at Weyanoke, Union engineers constructed a pontoon bridge 2,000 feet long. Engineers completed the massive bridge in eight hours, finishing just

Wilcox's Landing (LOC)

The pontoon bridge, at 2,100 feet long, was more than three times as long as the average bridge constructed by the army's engineers. (LOC)

before midnight on June 14. Immediately the artillery and wagons of the V, VI, and IX Corps began crossing. In the meantime, the II Corps was being ferried here at Wilcox's Landing. By midnight on the sixteenth, the entire Army of the Potomac was across, and the pontoon bridge was disassembled.

Moving the army south from Cold Harbor and crossing the wide river were major logistical challenges successfully overcome by the army's planners. Most of the troops crossed on steamships, the bridge being reserved for wagons and artillery. Wrote nurse Sarah Holstein, "In the evening signal lights were seen flashing upon the hilltops and from their camp grounds, the shipping was beautifully illuminated with various colored lanterns, and though in the midst of war, the river with its numerous lights, had a gay, holiday look."

Upon seeing the river, Lt. Col. Theodore Lyman of Meade's staff wrote: "Six weeks in the Wilderness, and the James river at Last!" No doubt many other officers and men were as relieved to reach this point. A Pennsylvania cavalryman noted, "The sight of that grand river—it was a splendid day—the gunboats, steamers and sailing vessels, was a novel sensation. We gazed upon the scene with as much joy and eagerness as if for the first time in our lives."

Wilcox's Landing today (RD)

Crossing the river revived the Union army's mood. Lieutenant Colonel Horace Porter noted: "The great bridge was the scene of a continuous movement of infantry columns, batteries of artillery, and wagon-trains. The approaches to the river on both banks were covered with masses of troops moving briskly to their positions or waiting patiently their turn to cross." It was, he said, "a matchless pageant that could not fail to inspire all beholders with the grandeur of achievement and the majesty of military power."

One Union soldier wrote, "A fine large plantation owned by Mr. W[ilcox] extends down to the river, and the oats and wheat, which it produces, show that the soil is much more fertile than that of the country. . . . Whatever will be the result of this campaign, Grant and Meade have shown themselves to be first class military officers."

Union surgeon George Stevens noted: "Near the crossing was a superb old mansion . . .surrounded by its little village of Negro cabins. Here many officers of the corps resorted to spend the time walking among the grand old trees or to stroll through the gardens, admiring the elegant and rare exotics which adorned the grounds. Within the mansion, we were met with the accustomed bitterness. . . ."

From Wilcox's Landing, naval vessels transported the bulk of the Federal army to the south shore of the James. In what must have been a moving scene, the XVIII Corps, on ships, passed by the II Corps, crossing here by ferry. Both units met up at Petersburg. (LOC)

Grant, observing the crossing with satisfaction, noted, "All effect of the battle of Cold Harbor seemed to have disappeared." One of Meade's aides saw the general break into a smug smile. "I think it is pretty well to get across a great river, and come up here and attack Lee in his rear before he is ready for us," the general remarked. Lincoln too had reason to smile, for although the campaign had cost the country dearly, he realized that the North was now much closer to victory.

"I begin to see it," he wrote in a telegraph to Grant. "You will succeed. God bless you all. A. Lincoln."

*   *   *

We hope you have enjoyed your tour. To continue following the armies south of the James River, turn left on the John Tyler Memorial Highway (Route 5) and drive seven miles to Jordan Point Road. Turn left there and follow the road across the river to James River Drive (Route 10). From there, follow signs to Petersburg National Battlefield and to Pamplin Park.

To head north toward Washington, turn left and follow Route 5 a distance of 10 miles to Interstate 295.

To visit Richmond, turn left and follow Route 5 a distance of 20 miles into the city. On the way, you will pass near other sites related to the Seven Days and Petersburg campaigns, including Malvern Hill, Deep Bottom, New Market Heights, Fussell's Mill, Fort Harrison, and Fort Gilmer. Many of these sites are part of the Richmond National Battlefield Park; others are preserved by Henrico County or the Richmond Battlefield Association.

Suggested Reading

THE 1864 OVERLAND CAMPAIGN

Davis, Daniel T. and Phillip S. Greenwalt. *Hurricane from the Heavens: The Battle of Cold Harbor, May 26–June 5, 1864.* (Savas Beatie, 2014)

Furguson, Ernest B. *Not War But Murder.* (Vintage Books, 2000)

Gallagher, Gary W., ed. *The Spotsylvania Campaign.* (University of North Carolina Press, 1998)

Gallagher, Gary W., ed. *The Wilderness Campaign.* (University of North Carolina Press, 1997)

Mackowski, Chris and White, Kristopher D. *A Season of Slaughter.* (Savas Beatie, 2013)

Mackowski, Chris. *Hell Itself: The Battle of the Wilderness.* (Savas Beatie, 2016)

Mackowski, Chris. *Strike Them a Blow: Battle Along the North Anna River.* (Savas Beatie, 2015)

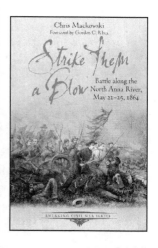

Matter, William D. *If It Takes All Summer: The Battle of Spotsylvania*. (University of North Carolina Press, 1988)

Rhea, Gordon C. *The Battle of the Wilderness, May 5–6, 1864*. (Louisiana State University Press, 1994)

Rhea, Gordon C. *The Battles for Spotsylvania Court House and the Road to Yellow Tavern, May 7–12, 1864*. (Louisiana State University Press, 1997)

Rhea, Gordon C. *To the North Anna River, Grant and Lee, May 13–25, 1864, 1864*. (Louisiana State University Press, 1997)

Rhea, Gordon C. *Cold Harbor, Grant and Lee, May 26–June 3, 1864*. (Louisiana State University Press, 2002)

Rhea, Gordon C. *To the North Anna River: Grant and Lee, May 13–25, 1864*. (Louisiana State University Press, 2000)

Simpson, Brooks D., ed. *The Virginia Campaign of 1864 and 1865*. (Da Capo Press, 1995)

Trudeau, Noah A. *Bloody Roads South: The Wilderness to Cold Harbor, May–June, 1864*. (Little, Brown and Company, 1989)

About the Authors

Robert M. Dunkerly is a historian, award-winning author, and speaker who is actively involved in historic preservation and research. He holds a degree in History from St. Vincent College and a Masters in Historic Preservation from Middle Tennessee State University. He has worked at nine historic sites and written ten books and more than twenty articles. He is currently a Park Ranger at Richmond National Battlefield Park.

Donald C. Pfanz worked for 32 years as a National Park Service historian, most of it at Fredericksburg and Spotsylvania County National Military Park. Born in Gettysburg, Pennsylvania, he is a founding member of the Association for the Preservation of Civil War Sites (now the Civil War Trust) and has written four books about the Civil War, including *Richard S. Ewell: A Soldier's Life* and *War So Terrible: A Popular History of the Battle of Fredericksburg,*

David R. Ruth has served as the superintendent of Richmond National Battlefield Park since 2008. His career with the National Park Service spans more than 40 years, including service at Fredericksburg and Spotsylvania, Independence, Manassas, and Fort Sumter. He holds a degree in history from Virginia Tech. Ruth and his wife reside in Hanover County, Virginia.